MW01434697

A Victorian Educational Pioneer's Evangelicalism, Leadership, and Love

Pauline A. Phipps

A Victorian Educational Pioneer's Evangelicalism, Leadership, and Love

Maynard's Mistakes

palgrave
macmillan

Pauline A. Phipps
University of Windsor
Windsor, ON, Canada

ISBN 978-3-031-13998-7   ISBN 978-3-031-13999-4 (eBook)
https://doi.org/10.1007/978-3-031-13999-4

© The Author(s), under exclusive licence to Springer Nature Switzerland AG 2023

This work is subject to copyright. All rights are solely and exclusively licensed by the Publisher, whether the whole or part of the material is concerned, specifically the rights of translation, reprinting, reuse of illustrations, recitation, broadcasting, reproduction on microfilms or in any other physical way, and transmission or information storage and retrieval, electronic adaptation, computer software, or by similar or dissimilar methodology now known or hereafter developed.

The use of general descriptive names, registered names, trademarks, service marks, etc. in this publication does not imply, even in the absence of a specific statement, that such names are exempt from the relevant protective laws and regulations and therefore free for general use.

The publisher, the authors, and the editors are safe to assume that the advice and information in this book are believed to be true and accurate at the date of publication. Neither the publisher nor the authors or the editors give a warranty, expressed or implied, with respect to the material contained herein or for any errors or omissions that may have been made. The publisher remains neutral with regard to jurisdictional claims in published maps and institutional affiliations.

This Palgrave Macmillan imprint is published by the registered company Springer Nature Switzerland AG.

The registered company address is: Gewerbestrasse 11, 6330 Cham, Switzerland

For Alan

ACKNOWLEDGMENTS

For the twenty-year archival journey that shaped and inspired this book, I first thank Dr. Deborah Gorham, my doctoral adviser in History at Carleton University, Ottawa, who encouraged my research into the relatively unknown English educational pioneer, Constance Louisa Maynard (1849–1935). My doctoral dissertation translated into my published biography, *Constance Maynard's Passions: Religion, Sexuality, and an English Educational Pioneer 1849–1935* (2015), which analyzes how faith shaped Maynard's crucial role in women's higher learning and passions for key loves in her life. In comparison, this new book emerges from my discovery of sensational new facts in the archive about Maynard's behavior as an educator, patriotic visionary, and pioneer student of psychology. Indeed, the unveiling of extraordinary micro-historical events caused by Maynard offers readers a rare window into a past subject's mindset. For example, how Maynard's bizarre longings for her student lover ruined the student's well-being and initial academic career. Yet Maynard's "mistakes" also provide new insight into Victorian concerns that, astonishingly, pertain to our current moment.

Certainly, serendipity in the archive inspires historians to ask new questions, and sometimes, revise former interpretations of the past. For this, I am grateful to former Queen Mary University of London archivist Anselm Nye, and Honorary archivist and historian Dr. Janet Sondheimer, who first introduced me to Maynard's numerous publications and unpublished diaries, autobiography, journals, and correspondence. Additional archival information in this book has been collected over the years from Girton College Cambridge, Bedford College London, the University of St.

Andrews Library Scotland, and Royal Holloway College London. In recent years, Queen Mary University of London Archive officers, Lorraine Screene and Florence Dall, have directed me towards the handwritten Council of Westfield Minutes and Maynard's newsletter, from which I discovered new information. They also made available many of the archival photographs in this book.

The invaluable contributions of research assistants Callum Murgu, Amanda Alchin, Matthew McLaughlin, and Alexander Cramer were helped by funding from the University of Windsor's Outstanding Scholar program and the Department of History. I also thank the four anonymous reviewers for helpful comments and individuals including Emily Russell, commission editor for history at Palgrave Macmillan, Tryphena R., project coordinator at Palgrave Macmillan, and Sugapriya Jaganathan, project manager at Palgrave Macmillan for their interest in this project and hard work in bringing it to publication. Last, my husband, Alan, has had patience and love over our many years together. My daughter and son, Dr. Kelly Phipps and Dr. Gregory Phipps, respectively, also have academic careers and publishing records that with their unique personalities are sources of pride for me.

Contents

1 Introduction — 1

2 Longing "for Excitement of Feeling," 1849–1871 — 23

3 Evangelical Prophet at Girton, 1872–1875 — 47

4 Difficult Relations, 1882–1891 — 73

5 Colonial Affairs, 1897–1904 — 99

6 "Noisy Rabble of Our Fears," 1917–1934 — 127

Bibliography — 153

Index — 161

List of Figures

Fig. 1.1 Constance Maynard aged thirty-eight, ca. 1888, with Bible in hand. Courtesy of Queen Mary University of London Archives/Westfield College/WFD. Reference WFD/25/1/1.   3

Fig. 1.2 Discarded page from Maynard's autobiography, written in 1915. Courtesy of the Queen Mary University of London Archives/Westfield College/WFD. Reference CLM/6/3/1. Notice the X in the margin and lines through comments at the top of page 341 that Maynard now possibly thought discriminatory. She had referred to Girton students R. Aitkin and M. A. Kingsland "as the first drops of the shower that ha[d] brought to so low a level of the refinement of … Women's Colleges." They had attended the new public middle-class girls' "Grammar (high) Schools" before Girton rather than the elite (upper-class) private boarding schools for girls.   14

Fig. 2.1 Constance Maynard's green book, 1869, page number 12 and 13. Courtesy of Queen Mary University of London Archives/Westfield College/CLM. Reference CLM/1/5. Writing at age nineteen, we glean Maynard's upbringing and conflicts. The first paragraph on page 12 concludes that "faith and prayer are really stronger than sin [worldliness], because Christ is stronger than Satan." The bottom of page 12 and the top of page 13 then ruminate upon a former Belstead student named Edith, and her sister Fanny, whose "evil" love of dancing, parties, and the theatre were encouraged by their "weak" parents. Fanny had died that autumn, and now apparently, Edith wondered "if Fanny would have done just as she did, had she known her end was near."   35

xii   LIST OF FIGURES

Fig. 3.1   (Left) Groups of early Hitchin students, ca. 1870. Louisa Lumsden is seated to the far right and Rachel Cook is seated next to her, with pioneers Emily Townsend, Isabel Gibson, and Anna Lloyd standing behind them. Lumsden and Cook were among the first women to complete studies in the Classics. Courtesy of St. Leonards School Archives, St. Andrews. (Right) Groups of early Hitchin students, ca. 1873. Amy Mantle, who would form a relationship with Maynard at Girton in 1874, is standing in the middle of the back row. Courtesy of St. Leonards School Archives, St. Andrews.   52

Fig. 3.2   Constance Maynard at Girton with fellow members of the Girton Bible meeting, ca. 1874. Maynard is seated on the left-hand side with her arm around Amy Mantle. Courtesy of Queen Mary University of London Archives/Westfield College/WFD. Reference WFD/25/ 1/1/1.   62

Fig. 4.1   External view of the back garden at Maresfield Terrace with the Westfield College group, 1889. Courtesy of Queen Mary University of London Archives: Westfield College. Reference WFD/25/3/4. This image of Westfield's "annual garden party" examples how middle-class college women negotiated femininity with the masculine corporate. As Constance Maynard as Mistress pours tea, her resident staff members, Anne Richardson, and Mabel Beloe, seem prominent in the BA academic dress as graduates of the University of London. Maynard was denied the gown and cap because she completed her studies at Oxbridge.   80

Fig. 4.2   External view of Kidderpore, the white neo-Classical stucco mansion to the far right, which became the "second" Westfield in 1891. Courtesy of Queen Mary University of London Archives/Westfield College/WFD. Reference WFD/25/3/1.   88

Fig. 4.3   Westfield College (at Kidderpore), 1894, showing the group of forty eight students and three lecturers. Maynard, who particularly disliked Westfield's "secularist" ionic columns, is seated in the middle of the first row wearing her white lace cap. Courtesy of Queen Mary University of London Archives/Westfield College/WFD. Reference WFD/25/3/1.   89

Fig. 4.4   Early Westfield College Group, 1885, at Maresfield Terrace, at full capacity with eighteen students, three Resident staff members, and Maynard, aged thirty-six, who is center of the second row. Kate Tristram is to Maynard's left, and staff member Frances Gray is to her right with a book on her lap.

Fig. 5.1	Courtesy of Queen Mary University of London Archives/Westfield College/WFD. Reference WFD/25/3/1.	92
	Constance Maynard aged forty-eight, 1897, seated at her desk in the Mistress's room. Courtesy of Queen Mary University of London Archives/Westfield College/WFD. Reference WFD/1/1/2.	105
Fig. 5.2	Constance Maynard aged forty-nine, 1898, with Westfield group. Maynard is seated second row in center with long-term colleague Anne Richardson next to her on her right. Possibly, Marion Wakefield is seated next to Anne Richardson. The young woman resembles Maynard's description of her, was Richardson's niece, and did enroll at Westfield in 1898. Courtesy of Queen Mary University of London Archives/Westfield College/WFD. Reference WFD/25/3/1.	106
Fig. 5.3	Constance Maynard aged fifty-six, 1905, wearing her black preaching dress with Bible in hand. Courtesy of Queen Mary University of London Archives/Westfield College/WFD. Reference WFD/1/1/5.	116
Fig. 6.1	Westfield College (at Kidderpore) Dining Hall, undated. Courtesy of Queen Mary University of London Archives/Westfield College/WFD. Reference WFD/12/10/1.	132
Fig. 6.2	Students in attic Laboratory, Westfield College (at Kidderpore), c. 1916. Courtesy of Queen Mary University of London Archives/Westfield College/WFD. Reference WFD/25/4/2.	133
Fig. 6.3	Constance Maynard aged eighty-five, 1934. Courtesy of Queen Mary University of London Archives/Westfield College/WFD. Reference WFD/25/1/1.	144

CHAPTER 1

Introduction

Abstract Chapter 1 introduces readers to the extraordinary yet relatively unknown English late-Victorian educational pioneer, Constance Louisa Maynard (1834–1935). The author focuses on Maynard's privileged but ascetic upbringing and how larger ideas about class, gender, and empire shaped her life. Maynard is further contextualized in a discussion about the era that includes the importance of categories like class and new terms like agnosticism and sexology. Maynard's unique studies in the human mind are mentioned alongside her participation in the powerful movement towards women's higher learning. The structure of the manuscript is then outlined in discussion on the historian and the archive, historiography, and microhistory. Also discussed are the themes and theories used to analyze nine extraordinary microhistorical events caused by Maynard that illuminate her mindset and that of a society in tumult over femininity, sexuality, faith, empire, and science.

Keywords Historiography • Microhistory • Terminology • The Archive • Queer theory

In 1902, Constance Maynard, aged fifty-three, wrote a confession in her newsletter to former students:

> My Dear OS [Old Students], I'm [Constance Maynard] sorry to say that I have been quite sick of late and have requested a Leave from College. I feel the awful tension of real anxiety in those around me, rather as if a whole mass of duty is left to me, but I had transgressed a good deal this time, and it went rather near the edge.[1]

She had found the courage to tell her former students about her wrongdoing: "The awful tension" at college resulted from her "duty" as an educational pioneer and a devout Evangelical. As Maynard sadly explained, duty "went rather near the edge" when worldly feeling intervened, to cause "mistakes" that at their extreme caused "wrongs." In this instance, she admitted, "I had transgressed a good deal."[2] This book explores nine enigmatic actions motivated by Maynard's quests for educational leadership, global conversion, and love. In so doing, her story unfolds to expose a reflective past that might otherwise be overlooked. Maynard's mistakes challenged her faith and caused enmities with administrators and college women. Some of her college lovers even suffered emotional breakdowns. Yet amid her trials, Maynard made key decisions about her public and private life. Moreover, her so-called mistakes astonish as new insights into the rapidly changing world in which she lived.

Although she is quite unknown, the late-Victorian Maynard (1849–1935) is mostly remembered for her innovative Westfield College in London, England, which produced the first female BAs in the mid-1880s. Her work contributed to the success of a great national movement called the "cause" that demanded women's rights to higher education. Yet she remained forgotten until a former Westfield student and friend, Catherine Firth, published *Constance Louisa Maynard: Mistress of Westfield College* (1949), which paid attention to Maynard's conflict between science and faith.[3] Nothing about her was published after Firth's biography until 1982, when Maynard was included in the scholar Martha Vicinus's ground-breaking examination of college women's friendships.[4] Even so, Maynard remains absent in textbook writing on the cause. Nor does she feature as a prominent Evangelical or a pioneer student of psychology. In 2012, the digitization of her green book diary and autobiography inspired some writing that predominately analyzes her intimate Westfield college relationships.[5]

My previous research on Maynard, which included a biography published in 2015, is by far the fullest study of her life. Readers may thus question why another book about this elite white woman is justified, especially given the push for more diverse women's history. Certainly, diversity is important, but so too is history that challenges facts. This book sprouted from astonishing new information I uncovered about Maynard's experiences as an educational pioneer, Evangelical visionary, nationalist, and specialist of the psyche. In addition to new content and new arguments, my approach to Maynard's life vastly differs from that in my biography. *Maynard's Passions* was typical to the genre of biography, profiling how Maynard's important role in women's higher education and Evangelicalism shaped her professional ambitions and passions for key loves in her life.[6] In contrast, this book, written in the genre of microhistory, unveils tiny actions by Maynard that not only offer rare insight into her rationale for these. Her acts elucidate previously unknown facts about Victorians that pertain to our current moment (Fig. 1.1).

Fig. 1.1 Constance Maynard aged thirty-eight, ca. 1888, with Bible in hand. Courtesy of Queen Mary University of London Archives/Westfield College/WFD. Reference WFD/25/1/1.

"REASON" AND "CONSCIENCE"

Historiography about the minutia (as all history writing) is more refined than establishing facts or dates about a past. The goal is to answer the challenging "why" to emphasize the impact of an event or person. We might argue that while historians of women have explained how "the cause" forged new concepts of women's educational abilities, globally, Maynard's assurance that women had "both reason and conscience," bespoke the moment in history.[7] She knew the seeds of change were clear in 1869 when her mentor, Emily Davies asked society: "If a liberal education equips boys for all walks of life, why is it *less* suitable for young ladies? … The education of daughters from the labouring classes is as carefully watched over as boys, why is the case altered a few steps higher on in the social scale?"[8] Davies may have exaggerated what was for the labouring classes a rudimentary education, but she wished to expose gender-based education for the middle classes. In her view, girls' four-year training in "female accomplishments" for homelife was negligible, when compared to boys' eight-year education in the humanities and sciences for professional life. In fact, Davies's annoyance over Victorians' dismissal of "female capabilities" drove her to initiate Girton, the first women's college attached to Cambridge university that promulgated change.[9]

Davies objected to her patriarchal society that ranked upper-class white men superior to women, men of lower socio-economic means, and non-white individuals. Thus, Maynard's impressive homage to the cause, *We Women* (1913), was a brave challenge to historical misogyny: "Man, as a Race, has used us [women] *very* badly, accounting (us collectively) as hopelessly inferior to himself."[10] Her criticism bespoke centuries-old myths about women's physiological feebleness that had serious ramifications for Victorian women. Denied most social, political, and economic rights, prescriptions of femininity rendered women subservient to men. In 1869, Davies timidly beseeched society's support of women's higher learning: "It [Girton college] is not directed towards *changing* the occupations of women but securing what they do well." Thirty-four years later, however, Maynard's *We Women* declared: "Despite subjugation, women *have* the natural power of reason."[11] She was among the few courageous women to attend Girton in 1872, and one of the first Victorians to study the "Mental and Moral Sciences." She was as remarkable as the "First Mistress" of Westfield College which opened in 1882 with two notable aims: provide women with new opportunities to gain university degrees and send educated women to evangelize the increasingly secularist world. When Maynard retired in 1913 at age sixty-four, over 500 Westfield graduates had entered new female professions such as social work, university teaching, medicine, and missionary work.[12] The occupations of women had vastly changed.

To Maynard, women not only had the power of reason. *We Women* dwelled upon women's gift of "conscience; a source of knowledge guided by God."[13] Her concept of female piety invoked dynamic "moral keepers of the hearth" who preached Evangelical life-principles. Certainly, it was an era of "crisis in faith." Charles Darwin's geological-biological *On the Origin of Species* (1859) challenged Biblicism with his new theory of evolution, which "proved" how the strongest species survived. Yet it was not until the 1870s that the scientific community and a few intellectuals even accepted evolution. As the historians, D.W. Bebbington and Boyd Hilton explain: "Religious feeling, biblical terminology, and *stress* on Christ's sacrifice on the cross permeated *all* aspects of [Victorian] thought." These elements that persisted until the 1950s could also dramatically alter over a short period of time.[14]

Mid-to-late-Victorian Evangelicals drew upon incarnational theology that exhorted Christians to "Rest in Faith" because Christ's Crucifixion had saved them from Adam's sin.[15] In stark contrast, Maynard's parents interpreted Christ's Crucifixion as a symbol of human failing: one must renounce the worldly and the carnal for personal salvation. Sadly, their refute of social activities and secularism instilled in Maynard troubling life paradoxes: she lived in opulence but must deny "worldly" parties or the theatre; she "longed for love" as she resisted such "carnality"; she believed "all [were] spiritually equal" yet was irrevocably class and (what we would call) race biased, and she studied science at Girton while claiming it was "evil." Moreover, underlying Maynard's conflicts lay an overwhelming responsibility, "religious duty." She thought herself a prophet, "Chosen by God to lead college women (and society) from worldliness towards salvation."[16]

In a sense, Maynard's religious duty mirrored Victorians' view that a passionate friendship among women in "search of God" was a part of female development. As historians of sexuality including Carroll Smith-Rosenberg explain: "Society permitted a wide latitude of sexual feelings between women."[17] At Girton, Maynard wrote unabashedly about the culture of female friendship:

> She knows my [Maynard] step and stands with outstretched arms as I enter with the almost painful longing expression that love must bring as it comes in force ... She says her world was empty before she met me; that she had often fallen in love before but *that* was hollow and worthless. She says I am her great treasure.[18]

Nevertheless, Maynard's inability to disavow love for God not only deepened her life paradoxes and sense of failure. Her conflicts were exacerbated by her life choices. Most middle-class women married men and maintained same-sex ties. However, if a woman dared to pursue a career, she faced social ostracization and forced singleness. In result, the lonely Maynard relied upon college women for professional and emotional well-being. Tragedies perhaps inevitably followed her relinquish of duty to pursue "worldliness."

"ENGLISHNESS" AND "THE MIND"

While Maynard's ascetic upbringing and educational milieu shaped her life, so too did an "Englishness" that interwove with her role as Mistress and prophet. Her nationalism not only resulted from Britain's vast colonial power over the Canadas (British North America), the Cape of Good Hope (South Africa), and New South Wales (Australia). Her wealthy father traded at the Cape, which accounted for 13.6% of Britain's total overseas trade. After 1870, however, Britain began to dwindle as a world leader, and Maynard was among the many who clung to an intense patriotism. In 1896, for example, Westfield students were reminded of their duty to "rightfully" maintain the British empire, and told: "Wherever 'England' comes, law and order begin!"[19] Many English people even felt superior to members of Great Britain, particularly the Irish who, like South Africans, were deemed incapable of self-government. Meanwhile, Maynard's vigor for missionaries at the Cape relayed British imperial interests, which created the greatest colonial war of the century.[20]

Maynard's patriotism and piety were ignited by her unique study of the "Mental and Moral Sciences" (human mind) at Girton in 1872. As the historian of science Roger Smith explains, this new field debated what it was to be human in a social world:

> Major intellectual innovations tied mind to nature: mental life to the brain and human nature to [Darwin's] evolutionary history. The claim that human

beings originate in nature... justified belief in the possibility of a science of human nature and hence a natural science [of what became] psychology [upon which] many placed high hopes.[21]

Maynard's exploration of Darwin's *Origin* and philosophers like John Locke introduced her to the notion that ideas were derived from one's sensation and experience. Her biggest challenge, therefore, was conceding that feelings were *hers* rather than actions to repress for God. Although Maynard's studies or "Tripos" challenged her faith-based sense of right and wrong, it played an astonishing role in her passionate, power-based relations with college women.[22]

Maynard's Tripos also forced her to confront her past. By 1925, her Tripos on the general laws of the (normal) human psyche had metamorphosed into "the psychology of the individual" understood through the pole of abnormality.[23] In Britain, the scientist Havelock Ellis categorized "normal heterosexuality" in opposition to "aberrant [all other] sex." Also influential were the ideas of the Viennese pioneer of psychoanalysis, Sigmund Freud. At age seventy-seven (1926), Maynard was shocked by the challenges to her late-Victorian culture of same-sex intimacy. The new psychologically based theories implied that she had engaged in abnormal relations with college women.[24] She sadly mulled her studies in the "Mental and Moral," and more particularly, her past same-sex acts and behavior(s) that were driven by her atypical professional role, her faith, and her Englishness.

....

Maynard's "mistakes" from her ascetic upbringing and unusual life choices proffer stunning insight into her mindset and that of her era. Her experiences as a Girton student in 1874, for example, provide novel insight into the "crisis of faith" that resulted from science like Darwinism. Victorians reacted through the physical developments of church buildings and the new Christian science that interwove biology and creation to challenge Darwinism.[25] Chapter 3 however, portrays a unique aspect of this social-physical milieu in Maynard's provocation of a science-faith division at Girton. In fact, this minute event astonishes, for it suggests that late-Victorians were more uncertain about faith than historians argue. History happens when we make new discoveries, ask new questions, and as a result, revise former interpretations of the past.

The same is true if we pause on Maynard's coax of fellow Girton student, Amy Mantle to embrace yet to resist their physical passion for God.

Maynard's behavior seemed at odds with the demonstrative female culture, but how might we explain it? It proves difficult because historians are wary of writing about women who dominated women using pain.[26] Chapter 3 tackles this sensitive topic through a careful micro-investigation of Maynard's actions to highlight *her* perception of how she treated Mantle, and why it influenced her future college bonds. Even more curious is Maynard's discomfort with Mantle's sensuality. She questioned same-sex feelings in 1875, which is over thirty years earlier than historians propose that society condemned such "deviance."[27]

Correspondingly, while much is written on how the cause dramatically altered women's lives, virtually nothing exists on how emergent professional educators *coped* with their new occupations within a patriarchal society. Chapter 4 addresses this lack, showcasing tiny events in 1882, 1884, and 1891 that illustrate Maynard's difficult Mistress-ship under her chiefly male administrators. More surprising, however, is Maynard's toxic relationship with a female Westfield Council member called Frances (Fanny) Metcalfe. In fact, their bitter relations expose heretofore unknown rivalry among the first female professionals. Readers learn of the Council's harsh retribution of Maynard for fifteen years due her "mistake" or outburst when the autocratic Metcalfe mocked her. Maynard was forced to be silent during an era that attributed professional competitiveness to masculinity.

Chapter 5, in turn, explores tiny incidents in 1898 and 1902 that illuminate how Maynard's nationalism and prophetism shaped her intimacy and subjugation of Marion Wakefield, an Irish Westfield student half her age. We carve a new trail to discover the peculiar ascetic roots of Maynard's beliefs in South African Calvinism. Sadly, Maynard's sense of power as Mistress, English, and prophet damaged Wakefield's health and self-esteem. Regardless, Maynard fully believed that Wakefield's crude "Irishness" was in dire need of "civilization" and conversion. Historians of empire among them Ann Laura Stoler highlight how a nationalist idea like Englishness was a medium "through which raced, sexed, and gendered bodies interacted with each other and with systems of domination … in both colonial and metropolitan contexts."[28] Maynard's relationship with Wakefield may appall us, yet it exemplified late-Victorian concern over "civilizing" and global control in the fin de siècle.

Meanwhile, the elderly Maynard floundered under new theories of the subconscious that infiltrated Britain in the mid-1920s. She particularly disliked Freud's and other budding psychoanalysts' idea that an "arrested stage in a child's psychosexual development" (like hers) could in later life enable

> excessively strong sexual excitations to find other outlets ... If, in the course of development, some [were] submitted to the process of repression which, it must be said, [was] not equivalent to their being abolished, the excitations continue[d] to be generated as before, but [were] ... diverted into other channels til they [were] expressed.[29]

Our concluding chapter outlines Maynard's painful reconsideration of her "misuse of love" when her former lover, the Irish Marion Wakefield, became a pioneer student of psychology and later, psychoanalysis. Virtually nothing is written on late-Victorian women who not only pioneered in studies on the mind but lived through vast changes in the field. Maynard left behind only brief thoughts on her Tripos and conversations about psychology and psychoanalysis with Wakefield in 1917, 1923, and 1934. Nonetheless, such minutia proves amazing windows into two late-Victorian women's extraordinary reflections on their intimate past due to their unique expertise in psychology.

A micro-analytical approach to Maynard's acts is critical in illuminating one late-Victorian woman's distinct experience of an era in tumult over femininity, faith, empire, and science. Readers likely know that the centuries-old genre of biography often featured important men's lives, but they may not be as familiar with the genre of microhistory forged in the 1970s. While budding social- and women's historians had in the 1960s challenged traditional largely male-based political history through innovative but overarching accounts of "workers," and "women," microhistorians asked big questions about small clearly defined events or individuals. István M. Szijártó describes the genre's fractal-like features: the microhistorian must first grasp "a mental picture" of an era to discern how an isolated event represents larger concerns.[30] I could not have written this book without first writing my biography. It was through my grasp of Victorians and one Victorian's memoirs that I detected anomalous events that seemed worth pursuing.

Discovering "the odd" is often the starting point of microhistory, which was introduced as an alternative historical method by pioneer Italian historians, among them Carlo Ginzburg. The peculiar comment, event, or phenomenon was taken as a sign of a larger, but hidden structure. Ginzburg and others like Natalie Zeman Davis usually employed a sensational court trial with a host of social data to redraw assumptions about the whole. Ginzburg's interest lay in illustrating the religious and social conflicts of sixteenth-century Italy through the perspective of a miller accused of heresy, while Davis relayed how a trial about impostership invoked among other things how an early modern French community judged proof. They explained their subjects' acts as life choices understood within the context of their society's sometimes-contradictory mores. In so doing, their microhistories challenged the traditional political metanarrative history.[31]

As the historians Hans Renders and David Veltman have recently noted, current studies in microhistory illustrate how the small reveals something new about the era, but also questions the event or individual as representative of the whole.[32] We mentioned that Maynard's acts denoted her culture and also disclosed new facts about it, some of which did not always characterize larger ideals like femininity. Microhistorians analyze the odd through various forms of data. For example, Kali Nicole Gros's, *Hannah Mary Tabbs and the Disembodied Torso: A Tale of Race, Sex, and Violence in America* (2016), employs a sensational trial to exemplify the biases of black justice in the 1800s. Meanwhile, Victor Bailey's, *This Rash Act: Suicide Across the Life Cycle in Victorian England* (1998), utilizes legal and medical literature to explain the phenomenon of suicide in a Victorian Yorkshire town.

Sigurður Gylfi Magnússon's, *Emotional Experience and Microhistory: A Life Story of a Destitute Pauper Poet in the 19th Century* (2020), examples those microhistorians who draw upon personal sources (in this case) of a poor nineteenth-century Icelandic man to highlight his perspectives on life and culture. *Emotional Experience and Microhistory* relays how the integration of diverse sources open up new perspectives on complex subjects.[33] This book also draws upon personal documents to illuminate how the small tells us more about the large. However, it does so through a series of tiny acts by Maynard throughout her life. Her extraordinarily massive archive relays the thought processes of an atypical female who challenged women's roles and conceived ambition and sex feeling through unusual faith and science-based concepts. Moreover, whether deliberately or not, Maynard wrote intriguing divergent accounts about the tiny acts that caused her shame. Chapters in this book are also quite unusual in that they begin with Maynard's life story, and then introduce a curious event caused by her actions and continue her story. Her acts are analyzed through pivotal concepts and historical methods that shaped historiography and yet, are particularly relevant to this microhistory. Let us further explain how Maynard's story was written.

THE ARCHIVE: DISCOVERIES, QUESTIONS, AND REVISING THE PAST

We have outlined how Maynard's nine "mistakes" disclosed new information about Victorians. Let us deliberate this statement by introducing her memoirs. Without doubt, her immense archive housed at Queen Mary University of London (QMUL) archives in London entices researchers with rows of tiny green and brown leather-bound diaries, a multivolume autobiography, numerous journals, public and private correspondence, and poems and sonnets.[34] Her earliest personal source was her green book (religious) diary begun in 1866 at age seventeen. She aimed to document her "Christian progress" but mulled her feelings in general, until her death at eighty-five. In 1871, when the green book became her "confidante," she initiated a parallel daily diary to jot down social events and public life at Westfield. Maynard planned to publish her autobiography that she inaugurated in 1915 at age sixty-six, but at over 1000 pages, it remained unfinished at the year 1902 when she died in 1935. In later life, she published books, tracts, and papers on religion, women's higher education, travel, nature, and social relations. QMUL holds various publications, including Maynard's powerful *We Women* (1910).

Maynard's green book was the most valuable source for this study. As a detailed "record of everything that touch[ed] [her] heart and soul," it proved inestimable, given Victorians' propriety about sex. Maynard was not only among the few Victorian women to leave records behind. Her green book was extraordinary in its frank discussions about sex. Moreover, her dilemma with same-sex feelings raised even more questions, for Victorians tolerated passion among women.[35] The green book also invoked what microhistorians call normal exception, that is, how an individual's life experiences convey larger social mores, but may also show exceptions to them.[36] Maynard's daily diary and travel diary were scant on detail and could be dismissed, yet both were crucial for this study. They disclosed fascinating clues about tiny events that the green book either ignored or downplayed. Though mired in cryptic language, these clues provided astonishing new facts about Maynard and her society. Her autobiography seemed a repetition of her diaries and journals. However, its hindsight interpretations of her past were striking; for example, her anachronistic use of the 1920s psychological term "repressive," to recall her late-Victorian upbringing, added an interesting layer to her life story.[37]

Maynard's circulatory newsletter or "budget" to former Westfield students was not only invaluable to this study. It proved a wonderful example of why this historian enjoys the archive and historiography. Prior to this book, I assumed Maynard's stated ignorance about psychoanalytical theory until 1926 at age seventy-seven, for I had no evidence to the contrary. However, on a recent research trip to QMUL to explore Maynard's newsletter, I uncovered her knowledge of the "new psychology" in 1904.[38] The language in the budget, thus, relayed Maynard's awareness of key developments in psychology and psychoanalysis over two decades earlier than she admitted in her diaries and autobiography. My find not only impacted my concluding chapter about Maynard's interactions with Wakefield. The newsletter illuminated more about Maynard's Tripos at Girton. My archival experience proved an important lesson. It reminded me that the historian should consistently question their preconceptions about the past. History happened when new evidence disputed "facts" in other sources I used to write Maynard's mistakes.

Terminology and the Language of Victorians

There are other ways that language interacts with sources to help explain the past. Maynard's Englishness, as mentioned, sanctioned her superiority over most others. Let us also consider the term "Victorian" that English society introduced in 1850. Historians often caption the era around Queen Victoria's reign (1837–1901): the early-Victorian period ranged between 1837 and the late 1840s; the mid-Victorian one was in place by the 1850s; and the more unsettled late-Victorian period emerged in 1870, with the late-1880s being a time of long transition.[39] This division of time partially explains Maynard's experiences. Had she lived in the late 1830s and 1840s, her faith would have characterized early-Victorians' justification of economic depression and plagues as necessary trials on earth for salvation in the hereafter. Yet Maynard was raised among healthier and wealthier mid-Victorians who promulgated a more celebrative "Rest in Faith." Her life as a late-Victorian educational pioneer, however, reflected society's struggle with the spread of Darwinism; social unrest (working-class unionism); the loss of British global power; women's entrance into professionalism; and a science that challenged same-sex intimacy.[40] The idea of Victorian periods helps us to better understand Maynard's particular social, religious, and sexual conflicts within the context of her era.

Victorians themselves pioneered terms. When the late-Victorian English biologist Thomas Huxley (who was inspired by Darwin) coined agnosticism in 1869, his challenge of "unknowns" without scientific proof generated works like Christian science and later, the new psychology.[41] Darwinism and the idea of agnosticism certainly provoked Maynard's particular religious crisis at Girton in 1874. Nor is it surprising that religious doubt led Victorians to ground their sense of self through the concept of class. Scholars tend to interpolate class within other intersecting modes of analysis, yet it had a very strong categorical meaning for Victorians. Emily Davies, we recall, spoke of the labouring classes, and social distinctions within the middle class were pronounced.[42] Generations of the lower, middle, and upper-middle classes had climbed the social ladder from capitalist ventures. Most Victorians glorified upper-middle-class male capitalists whom they believed "took" Britain from the landed gentry. This elite male group promulgated a Christian-based ethic of hard work and respectability; forged Britain's reputation as the "workshop" and banker of the world; and adopted the liberalist-economic ideal of laissez faire.[43] This was in part true of Maynard's upper-middle-class father, Henry.

The wealthy Maynards distinguished themselves from the mass of the laboring classes comprised of skilled workers, labourers, and the destitute. They were snobbish, but most siblings were keen to help their local poor to "self-advance" through diligence, industry, and thrift. Late-Victorian prejudice was however evident in Maynard's classification of labourers as the "lower orders."[44] Also worth mentioning is Maynard's statement in *We Women*: "Man, as a *Race* has used us [women] very badly." She applied race to what we today call gender to critique the social roles attached to femininity and masculinity. When speaking of what we conceive of as race, she turned to class and Biblical quotes to explain "God's natural distinction" between "good" elite Christian's and "the idle (evil labourer)."[45] Her concept was shaped by her father's self-identity as a white Christian South African trader who felt "superior" to the colonized pagan African tribes.[46] The introduction of the scientific term heredity, in the late 1860s, furthered Maynard's sense of entitlement. She did not perceive gender and race as we do, which reminds us of the perils of presentism in analyses of the past (Fig. 1.2).

Late-Victorians were as quick to reject terms. The new scientific study of sexology (later called psychology) that emerged in Europe in the

> Now all these who did the real work, has entered on a College course amid much laughter from their homes, & in some cases real opposition. Not R. Aitken & M. A. Kingsland, however. Both came from Yorkshire, & both represented the exceedingly hard working, resolute, ~~lower~~ middle class of that enterprising county. They came from old Grammar Schools, & pushed forward to gain the best they could out of the hard-won three years. It was a little bit crammy, a little bit sordid, & they were the first drops of that shower that has brought to so low a level the refinement of our Women's Colleges, but they were inevitable, & these two were good specimens. Every one of the others had come by their own strong desire after knowledge & training that should somehow make them of more worth in the world. Their spirit was indeed beyond praise in its love of learning for its own sake, & in a kind of lofty aspiration that this new departure, this great treasure suddenly laid in their hands, should be kept unblemished; the step forward was to be unconnected with anything political such as the Suffrage, on which there might well be two opinions, & was to eschew any motive but that of the noblest possible. All this feeling was powerfully embodied in S.J. Lumsden, & truly the College owes her a very great deal. We were determined to preserve sweet & genuine womanliness amid all our experience, to be unobtrusive in dress, and scrupulously modest & polite in manner, & looking back I think it was all rather wonderful that a dozen energetic lively creatures should, without the least external guidance, have been so thoroughly aware that the whole of this vast experiment depended on their corporate conduct.
>
> I do not see how the ethical feeling could have been higher, & the one real lack was Religion. With the high standard with which I came, there seemed to me to be none, though this took me long to find out, as

Fig. 1.2 Discarded page from Maynard's autobiography, written in 1915. Courtesy of the Queen Mary University of London Archives/Westfield College/WFD. Reference CLM/6/3/1. Notice the X in the margin and lines through comments at the top of page 341 that Maynard now possibly thought discriminatory. She had referred to Girton students R. Aitkin and M. A. Kingsland "as the first drops of the shower that ha[d] brought to so low a level of the refinement of … Women's Colleges." They had attended the new public middle-class girls' "Grammar (high) Schools" before Girton rather than the elite (upper-class) private boarding schools for girls.

mid-1860s opposed ideas of sexuality understood through faith. In England, the Church had long since condemned incest and sodomy, and Victorians, likewise, believed them to be crimes and the gravest of sins. Thus in 1897, when the English physician and sexologist Havelock Ellis introduced sodomy as a "biological anomaly," the few aware of him not only scorned his separation of sex from faith through science, they called obscene his *Studies in the Psychology of Sex* (1897) that codified "normal" sex as heterosexuality. This was not surprising since passionate friendship among women (and among men) was still a part of the culture. Yet despite opposition, Ellis inspired Sigmund Freud's and others' classification of sexuality based on the new theories of the subconscious.[47] The idea of non-heteronormative sex as a psychological irregularity eventually infiltrated society, but the question is, when?

Some historians, among them Roy Porter and Lesley Hall, argue that sexology/psychology had no impact until the 1940s. Others counter that a few budding psychologists who conceived same-sex desire as a sexual preference in the mid-1920s openly challenged heteronormative society.[48] What do Maynard's records tell us? She never mentioned Ellis or sexology, but as we know, she did pioneer in human thinking in 1872; knew of developments in the new psychology in 1904; and in 1926, was affronted by psychoanalysts whom she "*suppose[d],* would call [her] past feelings 'a thwarted sex instinct.'" What she had considered friendship with college women in the mid to late 1870s, 1880s, and 1890s was now termed abnormal. She was confused because she had always understood sex feelings in relation to men.[49] Yet her Tripos at Girton had inspired her to explore same-sex sexual self-consciousness at least thirty years before psychological theories took hold. Her fascinating life experiences help us to better understand one individual's complex process of moving from religious to scientific understandings of sex.

WRITING THE SENSATIONAL TALE

Sensational stories about the past intrigue us and influenced those living before us. Historians often cite the ancient Greek, Herodotus, as the first historian who gathered evidence for speeches on military history. After Herodotus' gripping political tales came written history based upon the Judeo-Christian notion of God's "guide of human nature." Christian historiography continued until humanist thinking proposed that *people* created history.[50] We may not consider this information useful, but it does invoke the mindset of the time in which elements linger. For example, as a child, Maynard could only read history that emphasized God's workings on earth: "Life lessons from religious failings."[51] Yet paradoxically, her specialty at Girton exalted humanism. The nuances of past thinking help to explain the controversies that Maynard faced.

Today's historiography, as we know, can be controversial. Explanations about a past also vary, for example, in the historian's approach to a topic through a genre like biography or microhistory; historical field like women's history; or the use of theory from such disciplines as philosophy. Above, we discussed the genre of microhistory and touched upon the fields of women, sexuality, empire, and science to explain Maynard's experiences, but worth mentioning is the impact of fields on the discipline of history. Women's history, for example, established that "women" (and indeed any minority group) did not "simply add" to traditional history, but shaped it. The topic of sex, meanwhile, exampled how a field had to prove its "worth" and feasibility; budding historians of sexuality tackled subjectivity, asking: "Is sex an act, a category of person, or a practice?"[52] Carroll Smith-Rosenberg's "Female World" (1975) embraced this challenge by illustrating how passionate friendships among women "flourished in certain social structures amid different sexual norms."[53]

Some historians of women and sexuality found useful queer theory that entered academic discussion in the early 1990s. Queer pioneer Judith Butler dismantled overarching ideas like "gender" and "sex" to highlight that identity formation, while socially constructed, was fluid and multifarious rather than fixed and coherent. We adopt this perspective in our micro-analyses of Maynard's complex thought processes. Teresa de Lauretis and others' deconstruction of the binary model of gay/straight and man/woman was another key moment that shaped historiography. *Differences* between subjects/persons, rather than universalized commonalities became critical in studies on the past.[54] A queer approach to Maynard's self-formation highlights the fluidity of gender, desire, and sex, but also warns us against reifying and projecting current hetero and homosexual identities onto her past.

Although we utilize ideas from historical fields and queer theory, this book does not dwell on them. Rather, they reinforce our methods sections that highlight intriguing concepts from mentalité and the linguistic turn that profoundly shaped historiography, but yet are conducive to this micro-analysis of tiny sensational acts. Readers are also privy to intriguing microhistory methods that include incident analysis, the evidential paradigm, and the singularization of history, which augment our analyses of intriguing clues and puzzles. Readers will undoubtedly recognize that the juicy parts of Maynard's experiences are told in the historiographical sections and through intriguing mysteries. Needless to say, our interpretation of Maynard's acts through genre, field, theory, and microhistory methods signify that historiography is biased. Moreover, since much of history (including Maynard's) was not recorded, history writing is by extension partial and discontinuous. This does not imply that historians lack skills. After all, in the late 1800s, the German Leopold von Ranke academicized history by disentangling it from literature; he argued that the historian's scrutinization of sources led to accuracy about a past.[55] Most historians today accede that "facts" may be ascertained through consensus, even if scholars interpret facts in different ways.

The idea of history as partial but factually verifiable also inspires us to heed the range of voices in personal documents. Facts in Maynard's memoirs belie each other yet still build upon her past. Her documents also suggest that while parts of Victorians' legacy remain with us—for example, what we call gender and race discrimination—Victorians were not like us. We have noted how Maynard's use of the word race was conceptually different from ours. This sort of fact finding is important, and we address it throughout this book. But what if we cannot verify a fact? What if a remark seems anomalous to the time? Chapter 2 introduces the possibilities of this fascinating challenge. Some historians argue that past "strangeness" provides a valuable perspective on the present. Others surmise that scholars can recover history by "stepping into past people's shoes" to see the world through their eyes.[56] Since we adopt both positions, we may propose that history is not the past, or even sources left behind. History happens when we authenticate sources; place them in historical context; and assess them before making arguments.

Historians should also consider what past authors intended. When Maynard secured former student and friend Catherine Firth as her biographer, she advised Firth to "speak the truth in love, [adding], what I shared with others ... must not [be] hidden here." Firth decided that Maynard's emotional struggles were "too painful for a stranger's eye to read," but I think Maynard wished them to be known.[57] After all, she was a pivotal figure in women's right to higher education. Her story provides a clear entry point in which to explore the dramatic changes in a society's concepts of femininity and women's societal roles. Her life-long struggle with her faith and "calling" is also a fascinating avenue into the overlap between religion and science in the period. As compelling is how Maynard merged her elitist imperialist faith with her unique knowledge of psychology to express same-sex feelings. During a time of profound change, Maynard's conflicts caused strife and scandals at Girton and Westfield. These tiny events, hidden in her archives, are precious, for they were never publicly known. They are situated at the center of her story, not to slander Maynard but to showcase the particularity of a past and the remarkable difficulties that she experienced. The hope is that readers will better understand Maynard's mistakes, refracted as they are, through the lens of her life, for from them, Maynard not only helped to carve for western women their freedoms, her mistakes proffer extraordinary insight into one late-Victorian woman's thought processes.

Notes

1. Constance Louisa Maynard, *Budget Newsletter*, 1902, Special Collections, Courtesy of Queen Mary University of London Archives/Constance Maynard/WFD. Reference WFD/26/1/2. Hereafter cited as *Budget* with date.
2. *Budget, 1902*. Maynard's budget newsletter resembled that used by Methodists. Budget members who were former Westfield students placed letters about their families, careers, and so on in a little pouch that was circulated around, and then replaced by new letters. See also Constance Louisa Maynard, *Unpublished Autobiography*, Part I, Chapter 1, "1849–60," 6, written in 1915. Special Collections, Courtesy of Queen Mary University of London Archives/Constance Maynard/CLM. Reference CLM/PP7/6. Hereafter cited as *A*, plus part, date, page, and years written.
3. Catherine B. Firth, *Constance Louisa Maynard: Mistress of Westfield College* (London: George Allen and Unwin, 1949).
4. Martha Vicinus, "One Life to Stand Beside Me: Emotional Conflicts in First-Generation College Women in England," *Feminist Studies* 8 (1982), 603–627.
5. A Symposium at Queen Mary University of London, in London, UK in 2012, to celebrate the digitization of Maynard's green book diary and autobiography, inspired seven articles about Maynard that were published in *Women's History Review, Special Issue*, 25, 1 (2016).
6. See Pauline Phipps, *Maynard's Passion: Religion, Sexuality, and an English Educational Pioneer 1849–1935* (Toronto: University of Toronto Press 2015); Phipps, "Faith, Desire, and Sexual Identity: Constance Maynard's Atonement for Passion," *Journal of the History of Sexuality* 18, 2 (2009),

265–286; and Phipps, "Constance Maynard's Languages of Love," *Women's History Review,* (2016), 17–34.
7. See, for example, Martha Vicinus' *Independent Women: Work and Community for Single Women 1850–1920* (London: Virago Press), 1985, which exemplifies how early-Victorians' conception of women's role as teachers as extensions of "femininity" contrasted late-Victorians fear that qualified teachers threatened female domesticity.
8. Emily Davies, *Thoughts on Some Questions Relating to Women, 1860–1908* (Cambridge: Bowes and Bowes, 1910. Reprint, New York: Kraus, 1971), 102–103.
9. Davies, *Thoughts,* 103. For good discussion on the middle class see, Leonore Davidoff and Leslie Hall, *Family Fortunes: Men and Women of the Middle Class 1780–1850* (Chicago: University of Chicago Press, 1991). For more on girls' accomplishments such as piano playing and basic reading and math, see Deborah Gorham, *The Victorian Girl and the Feminine Ideal* (Bloomington: Indiana University Press, 1982). Middle class refers to members of the lower, middle, and upper-middle-classes.
10. Constance Louisa Maynard, *We Women: A Golden Hope* (London: Morgan & Scott, 1913), 130.
11. Davies, *Thoughts,* 102–103; and Maynard, *We Women,* 130.
12. For more about Westfield College, see Janet Sondheimer, *Castle Adamant in Hampstead: A History of Westfield College 1882–1982* (London: Westfield College, 1983), 22.
13. Maynard, *We Women,* 130.
14. Boyd Hilton, *Age of Atonement: The Influence of Evangelicalism on Social and Economic Thought, 1785–1865* (Oxford: Clarendon Press, 1988), 170; and D.W. Bebbington, *Evangelicalism in Modern Britain: A History from the 1730s to the 1980s* (Grand Rapids: Baker Books, 1989). See also, David Newsome, *The Victorian World Picture: Perceptions and Introspection in an Age of Change* (New Brunswick: Rutgers University Press, 1997), 15.
15. Bebbington, *Evangelicalism,* 22–44.
16. *A,* 1, 1, 4–12, written in 1915.
17. Carroll Smith-Rosenberg, "The Female World of Love and Ritual between Women, in Nineteenth Century America," *Signs* 1 (1975), 1, 25. For other pioneer work see Lillian Faderman, *Surpassing the Love of Men: Romantic Friendship and Love between Women from the Renaissance to the Present* (New York: William Morrow 1981); and Adrienne Rich, "Compulsory Heterosexuality and Lesbian Existence," *Signs, Journal of Women in Culture and Society,* 5, 4 (1980), 631–790.
18. Constance Louisa Maynard, *Green Book Diary,* 22 March, 6 September 1883, 69, Special Collections, Courtesy of Queen Mary University of London Archives/Constance Maynard/CLM. Reference CLM/PP7/2. Hereafter cited as *GB,* with date and page numbers.

19. *Budget* 28 May 1896; and 22 January 1906. For empire, see Andrew Porter ed., *The Oxford History of the British Empire: The Nineteenth Century* (Oxford: Oxford University Press, 2009), 15–25.
20. Constance Louisa Maynard, *Travel Diary*, 1900, 7, Special Collections, Courtesy of Queen Mary University of London Archives/Constance Maynard/WFD. Reference WFD/14/1/3. Hereafter cited as *Travel Diary*, with date and page numbers. For Ireland see, Thomas W. Heyck and Meredith Veldman, *The Peoples of the British Isles: From 1688 to the Present* 4th ed., (Chicago: Lyceum Books, 2014), 454, 475–476.
21. Roger Smith, *Between Mind and Nature: A History of Psychology* (London: Reaktion Books, 2013), 11.
22. See, for example, *GB*, 20 June 1874, 100; and *D*, 18 June 1873, 88.
23. See *A*, III, 25, "My Last Term, 1875," 763, written in July 1917. For studies on the mind see Nikolas Rose, *The Psychological Complex: Politics and Science in England 1869–1939* (London: Routledge & Kegan, 1985), 17. In contrast to Britain's slow acceptance of psychology, places like Germany had already established laboratories, journals, and courses in psychology.
24. See Ivan Dalley Crozier, "Taking Prisoners: Havelock Ellis, Sigmund Freud, and the Construction of Homosexuality, 1897–1951," *Social History of Medicine* 3, (2000), 450; and *A*, V, 44, "Westfield 1882," 3, written in August 1926.
25. For a good overview of the period see Colin Matthew, "Introduction," in *Nineteenth Century: The British Isles*, ed., Colin Matthew (Oxford: Oxford University Press, 2000), 2–36.
26. See Laura Doan's debate about writing on female–female exploitation in *Disturbing Practices: History, Sexuality, and Women's Experiences of Modern War* (Chicago: University of Chicago Press, 2013).
27. For example, see Roy Porter and Lesley Hall eds., *The Facts of Life: The Creation of Sexual Knowledge in Victorian Britain, 1650–1950* (New Haven: Yale University Press, 1995), 189.
28. Ann Laura Stoler, *Carnal Knowledge and Imperial Power: Race and the Intimate in Colonial Rule* (Berkeley: University of California Press, 2002), 32–33; and Elisa Camiscioli, "Women, Gender, Intimacy, and Empire," *Journal of Women's History*, 25, 4, (2013), 141.
29. Sigmund Freud, *Three Essays on the Theory of Sexuality*, translated by James Strachey (New York: Basic Books, 1962), 103–104. See also, Crozier, "Taking Prisoners," 450.
30. Sigurður Gylfi Magnússon, and István M. Szijártó, *What is Microhistory? Theory and Practice* (London: Routledge, 2013).
31. Carlo Ginzburg, *The Cheese and the Worms: The Cosmos of a Sixteenth-Century Miller*, translated by John and Anne C. Tedeschi, (Baltimore: John Hopkins University Press, 1980); Natalie Zemon Davis, *The Return of Martin Guerre* (Cambridge, MA: Harvard University Press, 1983). Of note is that other pioneer works, such as Emmanuel Roy Ladurie's

Montaillou, Cathars and Catholics in a French Village, 1294–1324 (London: Scholar, 1978), had a different approach. Ladurie wrote a "total" history.
32. Hans Renders and David Veltman, "The Representativeness of a Reputation: A Third Wave in Microhistory," in *Fear of Theory: Towards a New Theoretical Justification of Biography*, eds., Hans Renders and David Veltman (Leiden: E.J. Brill 2021), 191–195.
33. Kali Nicole Gros, *Hannah Mary Tabbs and the Disembodied Torso: A Tale of Race, Sex, and Violence in America* (Oxford: Oxford University Press, 2016); Victor Bailey, *This Rash Act: Suicide Across the Life Cycle in Victorian England* (Stanford: Stanford University Press, 1998); and Sigurður Gylfi Magnússon, *Emotional History and Microhistory: A Life Story of a Destitute Pauper Poet in the 19th Century* (London: Routledge, 2020).
34. To access Maynard's digitized "green book diary" and unfinished autobiography, visit http://www.library.qmul.ac.uk/archives/digital/constance_maynard.
35. A, I, 1, "1849–60," 2, written in 1915. For a firsthand account of Victorians toleration of passion among women see Frederick Saunders, *About Women, Love, and Marriage* (London: G.W. Carleton, 1868).
36. See Magnússon and Szijártó, *What is Microhistory?* Giovanni Levi, "On Microhistory," in *New Perspectives in Historical Writing 2nd ed*, ed., Peter Burke (University Park: Pennsylvania State University Press, 2001), 97–120; and Ginzburg, "Two or Three Things," 20.
37. See *A*, II, 4, "Adolescence 1865–66," 59, written in 1925.
38. See *Budget*, 1904.
39. Matthew, "Introduction," in *The Nineteenth Century*, ed., Matthew, 37–38.
40. See Bebbington, *Evangelicalism*, 22–40; and Hilton, *Age of Atonement*, 170–177.
41. Patrick Bratlinger, *Dark Vanishing: Discourse on the Extinction of Primitive Races, 1800–1930* (Ithaca, NY: Cornell University Press, 2003), 188.
42. For more on this argument see Carolyn Betensky, "Concept of Class in Victorian Studies," in *The Routledge Companion to Victorian Literature*, eds., Denis Denisoff and Talia Schaffer (London: Routledge CRS Press, 2019), 11.
43. T.W. Heyck, *Transformation of Intellectual Life in Victorian England* (Chicago: Lyceum Books, 1982); and Matthew, "Introduction," in *The Nineteenth Century*, ed., Matthew, 37–38.
44. Constance Louisa Maynard, *Daily Diary*, 6 September 1872, 22, Special Collections, Courtesy of Queen Mary University of London Archives/Constance Maynard/CLM. Reference CLM/PP7/2. Hereafter cited as *D*, with date and page numbers. For more on class and society, see M.J. Darnton, *Progress and Poverty: An Economic History of Britain 1700–1850* (Oxford: Oxford University Press, 1995).

45. Maynard, *We Women*, 130.
46. See *D*, 31 December 1904, 365; 3 July 1871, 23; and 26 March 1867, 52. For more on race see Porter, *British Empire*, 1–31.
47. Havelock Ellis, *Studies in the Psychology of Sex* (Harvard: F. A. Davis, 1897); and Sigmund Freud, *The Standard Edition of the Complete Psychological Works of Sigmund Freud*, translated by Alan Tyson (London: Hogarth Press, 1955).
48. Compare Porter and Hall, *Facts of Life*, with Susan Kingsley Kent, *Making Peace: The Reconstruction of Gender in Interwar Britain* (Princeton: Princeton University Press, 1993).
49. *A*, V, 44, "Westfield 1882," 3, written in August 1926.
50. See Fritz Stern's seminal, *The Varieties of History: From Voltaire to the Present 2nd ed.* (New York: Vintage Books, 1973), 13–16, 72–80. St. Augustine's *City of God* (413–426) held sway until works such as Niccolo Machiavelli's *The Prince* (1532) claimed "*people* always have been animated by desires."
51. See for example, *A*, I, 3, "1863–64," 59, written in February 1915; and 44, "Westfield 1882," 3. written in August 1926.
52. For early work on women's history, see, for example, M.C. Bradbook's study on Girton College, *That Infidel Place* (London: Chatto and Windus, 1969). The inauguration of *Frontiers* and *Signs* and the Berkshire Conference showcased women's history. In Canada, the first classes in women's history were offered at Carleton University and the University of Toronto in 1871. For discussion on the formation of the history of sexuality, see Jeffrey Weeks "The Social Construction of Sexuality," in *Major Problems in the History of American Sexuality*, ed., Kathy Piess (Boston: Houghton Mifflin, 2002), 2, 3–6.
53. In "Female World," 3, Smith-Rosenberg also provokingly wrote: "It is one aspect of the female experience which … we have chosen to ignore." For more on race see Porter, *British Empire*.
54. See Judith Butler, *Gender Trouble*, (New York: Routledge, 1999), x–xxi; Teresa de Lauretis, *Queer Theory: Lesbian and Gay Sexualities*, (Indiana: Indiana University Press, 1991); and Chris Beasley, *Gender & Sexuality, Critical Theories, Critical Thinkers* (London: Sage Publications 2005), 164–167.
55. Ranke created university seminars that trained graduate students examine sources and discuss them (Stern, *Varieties of History*, 273–280).
56. For good accounts of the direction of historiography see John Tosh ed., *Historians on History 3rd edition* (London: Routledge Taylor & Francis, 2018), 19–37; and Jeremy D. Popkin, *From Herodotus to H-Net: The Story of Historiography* (Oxford: Oxford University Press, 2016), 133–140.
57. Firth, *Constance Louisa Maynard*, 5.

CHAPTER 2

Longing "for Excitement of Feeling," 1849–1871

Abstract This chapter details how Maynard's repressive upbringing shaped her unusual life. Most mid- to upper-middle-class Victorians believed that Christ's Crucifixion saved them from Adam's sin. In stark contrast, Maynard's parents interpreted the Cross as a symbol of human failing and advocated a life of worldly renunciation for personal salvation. Sadly, their beliefs instilled in Maynard troubling life paradoxes: she lived in opulence but must deny entertainment like parties typical of her class; she studied science at college even though she believed it an evil; and she longed for love as she resisted carnal feelings. Moreover, underlying her conflicts lay her overwhelming sense of being chosen by God to lead society from worldliness towards salvation. The chapter concludes with an intriguing clue that stemmed from Maynard's secret passionate bond with a female villager that contributes new information about Victorian women's sexuality.

Keywords Theology • Science • Historical Facts • Incident Analysis • Class • Nation • Gender and Sex

In 1868, the young Constance Maynard reminded herself about the perils of longing:

> I [God] will hedge up thy way with thorns that will wound you if you try to turn back to the old ways ... All I gave you that seemed so attractive was mine to give or withhold. Therefore, will I return ... and take away your gifts given to cover your nakedness ... I [Maynard] think God means us to summon the highest part of our being to control the lower parts.[1]

She had adapted this passage from Hosea in the Old Testament that solemnly addressed human sacrifice for sin. For the nineteen-year-old Constance Maynard, however, Hosea symbolized that feeling was as shameful as nakedness. She must not express pleasure in the usual activities of her class and gender such as dancing or heterosexual romance. Nor could she "moon" over a best friend.[2] This chapter examines how Maynard's upbringing impelled her to transgress an emotional world denied to her. Accounts of her childhood may appall us or lead us to question their veracity. Moreover, Maynard's archive itself confounds us with cryptic remarks and conflicted feelings about life; even so, from such contradictions we gain astonishing insight into her experiences and era. But what if we cannot verify a fact from her archive? We think her raptures over sex feeling are unusual. We think she tells us something extraordinary about a young Victorian woman's experiences. Can the obscure, the unverifiable, count as a fact? We are astonished to discover that it can.

Let us begin our story of Constance's upbringing from facts we can verify. According to Constance, her cousin Mary King, and her biographer Catherine Firth, the Maynard children were financially privileged but somewhat mired by emotional conflicts. Mary King, who knew Constance from birth, described her as a "happy, clever, and attractive child, with large luminous eyes and unusual golden-brown hair." Born on 19 February 1849, she was the second youngest of six children. Josephine, the firstborn in 1839, was followed closely by Harry in 1840. Gabrielle came along in 1845, followed quickly by Dora in 1846, and George in 1850.[3] The children lived during the stable mid-Victorian era (1850s–1860s) that benefitted the middle classes who prospered from laissez-faire economics and free market capitalism. The onset of mass marketing, in turn, disseminated moral values that were reflected in taxes, the classification of crime, and leisure activities. In short, this liberalization of the middle classes aimed to both shape and unify active citizens, such as the Maynard children's father, Henry.[4]

The middle-class Henry, who mirrored his ancestors in trade overseas, had gained his wealth by shrewdly investing in South African diamonds. His marriage into French landed gentry further empowered him. Although his wife Louisa's family was penniless, her genteel status propelled the Maynards into the upper-middle class. Henry as an elite male gained other important privileges among them, status as a landowner and new voting rights.[5] Powerful, and rich, Henry raised his family in luxury in the spectacular mansion, Oakfield, near Hawksworth village, in Kent, about sixty kilometers from the city of London. Constance's autobiography was a glowing testimony to a period that facilitated class mobility and sumptuous living:

> Life was idyllic indeed. I was attended by servants, nurses, and a governess. The field in front of Oakfield was yellow with buttercups and the gardens filled with lilies, azaleas, and scarlet geraniums. Beyond the back orchards were ponds, trees, and wild shrubbery, which eventually opened into Kent countryside. The grounds made it seem like a paradise for playing, climbing trees, making gardens, keeping pets and riding Fairy, our pony.[6]

In gentry-like philanthropic fashion, the Maynards oversaw the well-being of local, mostly poor Hawksworth villagers. Their children were tasked "to call on" villagers with baked goods and report back on illness or destitution. Other family activities evinced new upper-middle-class ideals such as those about leisure. There were "holidays to the sea;" an extravagant trip to France; and London city was accessible by train for shopping, visits to cathedrals, and newly built museums. Meanwhile, the innovative Crystal Palace that opened in 1851 introduced the Maynards "to the world" through the latest scientific inventions and economic achievements.[7]

Developments in global economics, middle-class liberalist-thinking, and scientific innovation constituted the mid-Victorian Evangelicalism that emphasized Biblicism and conversion. Historians characterize it as an omniscient middle-class mindset that eroded the power-based conservatism of the landed gentry. For example, the idea that wealthy entrepreneurs like Henry "ran Britain" justified middle-class economic and political power. Periodical literature that promulgated capitalism and nationalism also inspired in elite Victorians a keen interest in science.[8] The Maynards partook in such amateur pursuits as geology, botany, and physiology. Trips to London to see the latest science exhibition at the Crystal Palace were equally important. Constance was "fascinated by the electrical experimentation with wire."[9]

Yet, despite a life of privilege filled with interests, "childhood was forlorn," Constance lamented in her autobiography: "At the forefront of this loveless picture were my shadowy, stern, distant parents." Apparently, her father often traveled for business while her mother, "who took no delight in babies, or toddlers, kept to her two large rooms upstairs." Oakfield's typically delineated spaces for household members meant that Gabrielle, Dora, Constance, and George were raised in "the Schoolroom" by a variety of nurses and governesses who could be "very cruel and bad tempered." Constance's fearful accounts of a volatile nurse called "Jebb" implied they got "smacked by a rod" more often than kissed.[10] In addition, they dreaded their eldest sister Josephine whose

> talent for mockery and bullying frightened everyone. Even mother seemed frightened of her. There was often a slight tone of contempt, as if it were very kind of people to feed and clothe anyone who was worth so little, and on my [Constance] side a great fear lest I should provoke her to mimic or disparage me![11]

Fortunately, the young Maynards were "chums" in a family big enough to give scope for emotional outlet. Gabrielle, for example, told Constance that she was "precious and beautiful" to fend off Josephine's taunts. The children also distanced themselves from harsh authority figures through "make believe by becoming 'beings,' with a private language NOT to be understood by grown-up people. [They] even devised [their] own concepts and specific rules of conduct." Mary King thought "the game a curious affair which, played at every interval of the day, lasted about four years." However, Constance firmly told Catherine Firth that their "make believe was not a story, or a game, but a long systemic statement."[12] Whether a game or statement, they constructed a private world to counter their "public" one:

> I [Constance] remember that for over a year we wrote words on laurel leaves and threw them out of the window of the Schoolroom. One word would be Peace, another, Goodnight, and so on. One time, I remember that I wrote "God is *Love*," but I did not dare send it, for fear that it might be picked up [by our parents].[13]

Her memories suggested an unhealthy home life that repressed any form of emotion beyond that carved with siblings.

Unfortunately, sibling comradery only went so far. As the youngest daughter, Constance did not see her brothers and sisters for years at a time. Harry and George received a typical boys' education in the Classics and sciences before working for their father. They were away at an all-male boarding school for eight years. Meanwhile, Constance and her sisters entered the all-female Belstead boarding school at age fourteen for four years to train in "female accomplishments" for homelife. As one social critic sardonically observed: "Girls learn how to read and write, play the piano, and be *tolerably* skillful with a needle. Whether they also know French, how to spell, or work a sum is doubtful."[14] Constance's recollection of Belstead was as telling, but she was disappointed when "called home two years early to be schooled by three older sisters who had been educated till they were eighteen." She found solace in the advice of Belstead's kindly Headmistress: "Keep a green book [religious diary] to chart your Christian progress." However, the green book begun in 1866 relayed her thoughts in general: "Not a *word* of remonstrance [about leaving Belstead] did I make!" Her silence echoed mid-Victorians' opinion of girls' education and social roles: "I [Constance] was to feel *grateful* about becoming a grown-up daughter-at-home." She and her sisters felt obliged to read typical advice literature that claimed the "feminine qualities of passivity and subservience were *best* suited in the home."[15] They, like others of their gender and class status, were expected to remain home until married.

Rethinking Forlorn: "A Sort of Moral Torture"

Given social ideas on middle-class femininity, we cannot be surprised that Anglican tracts and sermons cautioned young women to maintain their "natural piety and humility by keeping out of life." The Evangelical movement within Protestantism followed suit with its three life principles: seek Biblical Truth; practice active conversion; and emphasize Crucifixiation.[16] The Maynard women as "moral keepers of the hearth" taught the Bible to local Hawksworth villagers. It was also a time when Charles Darwin's, Thomas Huxley's, and others' geological-biological based theories speculated how "a species" developed through the operation of chance, brutality, suffering, and extinction. A few scientists claimed that evolution theory explained the progressive, highly competitive world: "It was a beneficent process by which the nation got rid of its liabilities [paupers, infirm, incapacitated]."[17] Even so, most Victorians deemed evolution amoral and found respite in innovative Christian-geological theories: "We [the Maynards] find Mr. Darwin's evolutionary cycles useful," Constance explained: "His observing of stages: 1st, vegetative life; 2nd, creeping things; and 3rd, mammals (including man), correlate to the days of creation found in Smyrna, Rev. 2.8."[18] Christian science explained the transmutation of natural laws instituted by *God*. Ultimately, however, the Maynards and indeed most Victorians maintained revealed theology, or that based on scripture and religious experiences.[19] Biblicism remained a key part of life as society clung to Christianity.

The religious message in revealed theology depended upon the moral cultural climate. During the Victorian era, the Christians "guide for life" vastly modified between 1837 and 1850. The mid-Victorian period of stability, wealth, and rise in population was exemplified by the triumphant "Rest in Faith," which preached that *all* Christians could enjoy life. In the words of the well-known Anglican theologian Frederick Denison Maurice: humankind "never really stood in Adam as it *clearly d[id]* in Christ ... Christ redeemed us all because he never, unlike Adam, lost trust in God or tried to stand alone."[20] What about those who rejected this theology based upon the Incarnation? For the wealthy Maynards, it meant self-renunciation because humans "were born depraved" due to Adam's sin. The Christian must "shun the [mid-Victorian] world" of frivolity, decadence, and carnality for personal salvation. Certainly, earthly strife and transgress had helped early-Victorians to conceive social unrest, extreme poverty, and epidemics as "God's test of faith" for salvation. In fact, they believed that if Christians did not atone on earth, they faced eternal suffering in the Hereafter. However, the Maynards' belief in the Doctrine of the Atonement seemed antithetical to their lifestyle and era.[21]

Clearly, faith contributed to Constance's forlorn childhood. But who enforced such an austere and antithetical religiosity for the time? According to Mary King, Catherine Firth, and Constance herself, it was Louisa Maynard. In fact, Louisa did not marry Henry until she "believed him a Christian. He promised [and never did] interfere with her religious teaching." Henry's promise was not unusual, given the idea of female piety. However, Louisa's "search for moral conscience" opposed what she called, "the complacency of faith [incarnational theology]." We might think she condemned a theology that justified capitalism to the detriment of labourer's yet, asserted *all* could enjoy life. Rather, her "focus on God's bidding" led to a religious teaching that was cold, ascetic, and debilitating. From adolescence on, her children greatly suffered under her ban of usual activities "that aroused the senses" such as singing, parties, the theatre, and balls. Most social equals were deemed worldly and "not [their] sort." As a result, the interchange of visits and typical social life were non-existent.[22]

Louisa based her faith and life principle upon the Scottish Reverend Edward Irving's sermons that admonished "evil" worldliness such as sentiment, secularism, and materialist thinking. Equally curious was that not only mid- to late-Victorians but early-Victorians had denounced Irving's preaching, which seemed foreboding in general: "Evil tempted Christ, so God strikes terror in our hearts. He forces repentance by a sort of moral torture, into the bosom of despair."[23] Yet Irving's acceptance of gratified pain *resonated* with Louisa's life principle. As a result, Constance felt desperate and confused by her mother's warning that "feeling 'safe' in one's faith [was] more dangerous spiritually than a crime filled life. I remember I cried bitterly in my bed, not for any wrongdoing, but for what seemed so much worse, a general conviction of sinfulness and ignorance."[24] Given what Catherine Firth politely called, "the particular atmosphere of Oakfield," one can only imagine Constance's sense of failure about her inability to be unworldly and truly Christian. In fact, Mary King outright condemned Louisa:

> She [Louisa] would say, "*Being* good is not *good enough* for God." She sought to instill a careful exactness in everything they [children] did. Nothing demonstrative was permitted. At the time, I thought it was wonderful. Now I am not as sure ... The line between worldly feeling and faith might change as each child grew older, but none, I think, ever questioned its existence.[25]

Even as a child, Constance could not "admire the beauty of nature because [she] saw the line of 'demarcation' between the earth and heavenly blue sky."[26] At age sixteen, she struggled with an impossible quandary: "How does one know God through their mind rather than their emotions? I deeply fret about yielding to evil [emotional body]." In fact, she lamented at length about the

> *self-destructive* part which led to uncontrollable thoughts. You [Constance] *think* God is near in your *weakness* upon His love, but you *may* be treating Him like an earthly lover! This state of feeling is very worldly, and ...is very dangerous ... It can bring us great remorse because it drives us in shame away from God.[27]

To Constance, one only attained the divine body through blind obedience and humility. The Christian must not only relinquish self-approbation to find God. Any form of self-determination was evil. She would later tell readers that "Mother did [her] untold damage."[28]

A Sort of "*Moral Degeneracy*"

The above has conveyed how Constance's account of her upbringing led Mary King, Catherine Firth, and Pauline Phipps to consider it in part, within the context of Louisa's asceticism—King was privy to it. Yet, curiously, neither King nor Firth touched upon Constance's profound sense of superiority. Let us turn to her father. By mid-century, South Africa was Britain's largest empire and, indeed, Henry had made a fortune in South African diamonds, shipping, and banking. In fact, he typified those whom society claimed had assumed control of Britain from the gentry. As Firth explained, when back home, "Henry demonstrated competitive righteousness" through the cultivation of Hawksworth village workers. He built a row of cottages, a Schoolroom, and a Hall. The cottages were for those villagers who were infirm or without food; the Schoolroom was for the education of villagers and their children; and the Hall was built for Evangelical preachers to convert villagers or present lectures on the Bible.[29]

Yet despite his generous philanthropy, Henry was inherently prejudiced as a white colonist who had lived at the Cape of Good Hope during the 1820s. He conceived his "superior 'civility'" as human through ideas of "primitive" African tribespeople as "savages," which reflected the new thinking on civilization, population, and heredity. British scientists, intellectuals, and colonists alike were influenced by the predictions of the British clergyman Thomas Malthus, who in *Principle of Population* (1798) mathematically reasoned how overpopulation could outstrip food supply. Malthus' notion of "nature's brutal checks" like starvation or disease had not only impacted British thought on Poor Relief. His insights had led colonial governors to speculate upon the workings of colonization and predict that primitives could not survive if they opposed (white) civilization. Other works, such as Adam Smith's *Wealth of Nations* (1776), were similarly well regarded for illuminating European "hierarchy" through the link of economics with social organization and the "character" of people. Whether Henry knew of Malthus or Smith or was involved in debates is uncertain, but his colonial milieu was counterposed with tribespeople's purported "gross practices and superstitions."[30]

During the late 1860s, and early 1870s, Henry's "civility" became class-focused in his revulsion of "moral degeneracy" created by British industrialization; factories had "given rise to the lower orders" who were diseased and engaged in vice and crime. Henry seemed to recall Malthus in his opinion that populations tended to increase beyond means of subsistence. He particularly reviled paupers "who could not feed mouths." He also possibly knew of Francis Galton's new "science of improving stock [eugenics];" Galton's *Hereditary Genius* (1869) warned that the "feeble," among them urban paupers, could "degenerate" cities through heredity and thus destroy Britain's population. Henry who fretted over the spread of "physiological and spiritual degeneracy" was not alone in his views.[31] The New Poor Law (1834) had forced the destitute into workhouses to "mend their ways," but it had caused dissent amongst the middle classes. While social reformers including John Stuart Mill questioned the Poor Law and a Doctrine (Atonement) that punished the innocent (poor), for Galton and other budding Darwinists,

> The theory of evolution [was] the doctrine of Malthus applied with manifold force to the whole animal and vegetable kingdoms. There [could] be no artificial increase in food or encouragement of reproduction ... Extinction and natural selection [went] and in hand ... The production of new forms of nature entail[ed] the extinction of old forms.[32]

The new science likely bolstered Henry's concept of civility, but it challenged Biblical Creation and so, he appeared to maintain his Biblical/Malthusian views on moral degeneracy.

Henry's biases strongly influenced Constance, who grew close to him in her early twenties. Her green book invoked her mother's faith in the declaration that "*all* [were] equal spiritually." Yet her daily diary, begun in 1871 to record social events, called labourers spiritually undeserving. At age twenty-two, her "disgust of degenerates' sloth, disease, and immorality" in cities became a common theme in her diary that continued throughout her life.[33] Meanwhile, social critics, among them Charles Dickens, vividly detailed the dreadful living conditions of the poor. Socialists, in turn, supported labour unions and demanded increased pay and better working conditions for labourers. In contrast, Henry hoped that the coal miners on strike in 1871 would "be *starved* into submission."[34] Moreover, that Constance supported his classist views set her apart from most of her family. Her sisters had empathy for Hawksworth villagers while her eldest brother, Harry, supported the London poor. As he angrily told her: "Our parents *fail* to apply their beliefs to matters of life. Father is *enraged* by my aid to the 'evil' [labouring-class victims of the cholera outbreak]." Constance "could not help but admit that Harry had a point."[35]

Constance's pondering underscores how a rich archive can unveil the individual's self-formation. Influenced by her mother's faith, and her father's elitism, she yet wondered at Harry's socialist-minded convictions. As the eldest son, he would inherit the family business and estate, but "the gentle Harry" did not seem patriarchal minded: "Politics were not discussed at Oakfield and so, Harry was keen to teach [his siblings] about world affairs." One green book entry detailed his powerful lecture on the Franco-Prussian war, while another described his "fret over the London cholera epidemic that afflicted 900 labourers."[36] As it turns out, Harry had more interest in the London poor than the family business and hoped that Constance would assist him. She agreed, but not surprisingly, their father forbade "such nonsense."

Constance certainly had empathy for what she perceived as Harry's

> gloomy acceptance of a career that he hated. His euphemistic accounts of his father's tyranny and boundless courtesy in not giving details [were] clear ... as he [tried] to follow the path carved out for him. He often wishe[d] he could run away but kn[ew] *she* [mother] w[ould] likely hunt him down if he ever did.[37]

The "hunted" Harry no doubt symbolized Constance's own struggles with her mother. However, as her father's daughter, she had no real interest in helping Harry with the poor. Nor could she condone his "carelessness over responsibility." She adored Harry, but she resented "lea[ving] Belstead early so that *he* could explore Europe with a private tutor." Belstead was her chance to flee Oakfield and experience "a warm, cozy domestic atmosphere; a cheerful 'busy ness' over all sorts of trifling matters; and a triumphant [incarnational] theology." Like other girls' schools, "lessons were not Belstead's strong point!" For instance, "when [she] earned the title, First Class student, [she] was told to set an example by keeping up a tidy room and appearance."[38] Even so, she left Belstead early, and Harry failed academically. Moreover, his later mishandling of the family business in 1898 bankrupted the family.[39]

"Ignorance in Love"

Given Constance's struggles as a female, her home life, and her oddly conflicted worldview, how did her family's values resonate with society's views on sexuality? Sex as we know is an especially sensitive conductor of cultural and religious influences, and Victorians did indeed conceive sex through distinctive forms of regulation. While advice manuals cautioned parents to avoid the "dangerous topic with the naïve [female] sex, a young man's lustful aggressive nature serve[d] him well in life."[40] This double standard of sexual morality allowed men's sexual flings before and after marriage. How did Constance's writing echo these ideals? She first characterized females as "humble, passive, and fearful." She then told readers that her sexuality was awakened through "peeks at novels, and shy glances at the nudes at the Royal Academy ... The sensuality 'of the kiss' in Tennyson's 'Fatima' explained [her] excited feelings towards male cousins." When she "dared to make eyes at a boy, vivid words" from her sister Josephine warned that no respectable eighteen-year-old flirted with men. Meanwhile, her observation, "Harry *is* good [religious], but he is *known* to 'like a laugh and a pretty girl,'" seemed representative of prescriptions on male sexuality.[41] So far, Constance's views and experiences seem typical for a mid-Victorian female.

Regardless, society encouraged women to merge piety and passion in "gush and moon" over friends, even after marriage to men. Prescriptive writing like Frederick Saunders' *About Women, Love, and Marriage* (1868) seamlessly intersected passion among women with femininity, masculinity, and male–female sexuality; Dinah Mulock Craik's *Thoughts About Women* (1858) told women to form female bonds and "assign [themselves] *contentedly* into the hands of their husband;" and novels too, depicted female friendships that operated to assimilate heroines into conventional roles. When we turn to life writing of the time, we discover that the journalist Eliza Lynn Linton and social reformer Beatrice Webb (like Constance) portrayed aloof, neglectful parents. They also recalled (sometimes sarcastically) the "gay life in London [balls, dances, and parties]" and their marriage to men.[42] These well-known female writers seemed frustrated by gender mores, but sentiment was a part of their lives. In stark contrast, Constance, aged nineteen, "sincerely hope[d] that [her] long for excitement of feeling [would] pass." She also felt bitter, telling readers: "I deeply resent my ignorance in love! Friendship and Marriage are such great things. *Must* love be forever hidden away?" She and her sisters "had no London season, no parties, and no possibilities of love affairs."[43]

Whether deliberately, or not, Louisa raised her daughters to be spinsters; only one married and not until she was thirty. In later life, when Constance "met men whom [she] thought splendid, [she] always thought, why did *we* never meet men like this when we were younger?" However, she felt particularly desperate as a teenager. Her siblings were either away at boarding school or had left home, and sadly, she had no outlet in novels or outpourings to girls of her own age. When her father left for South Africa, her mother took a house in Highbury, London, to "keep an eye on Harry." Constance spent "long hours alone in a dingy little back room where [she] was supposed to do lessons." The autobiography continued: "Of all us girls, I got it the worst. I was alone, but she [mother] was ever vigilant, and only seemed happy when I read the Bible." When Constance finally formed friendships at Belstead, her mother quickly curbed them. Not only could she not see her friends, she could not even send them letters if her mother deemed them sentimental. Her one escape from her ascetic life was the garden: "There was a sheltered, winding path at the foot of apple-orchard and there, [she] measured off the furling. It was somewhere a trapped tiger could pace up and down. It was a real boon" throughout adolescence and young womanhood (Fig. 2.1).[44]

Historians and the Archive: When is a Fact not a Fact?

King's, Firth's, and Phipps's assessment of Constance's upbringing certainly invoke sympathy and raise questions. We may propose that their consensus over aspects of Constance's "forlornness" are facts. But what can we establish as "truth"? It is not an easy question to answer. We may find useful the historian Ludmilla Jordanova's view on historiography: "Truth and objectivity are not the most helpful concepts for [historical practice], reliability and judiciousness are more relevant." Jordanova's perspective on "the provisional nature of knowledge" does not of course demean the quality of historiography. She views fact-finding as fundamental to the historian's practice; however, as she points out, facts are inseparable from how historians interpret them.[45] Readers may think that King as a family cousin was critical of Louisa, Firth as Maynard's former student and friend wrote "kindlier" of the family, and that Phipps's interpretation

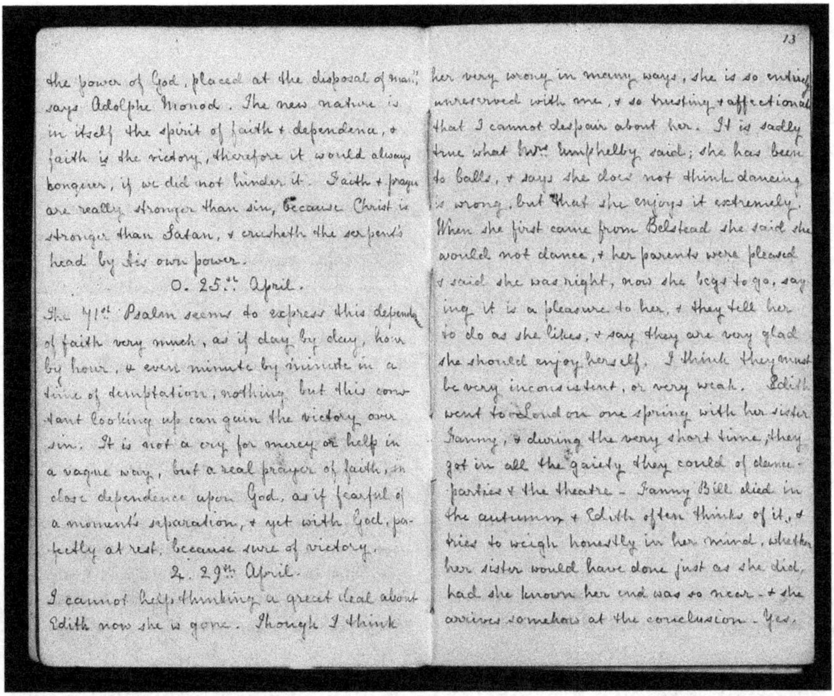

2 LONGING "FOR EXCITEMENT OF FEELING," 1849–1871   35

Fig. 2.1 Constance Maynard's green book, 1869, page number 12 and 13. Courtesy of Queen Mary University of London Archives/Westfield College/ CLM. Reference CLM/1/5. Writing at age nineteen, we glean Maynard's upbringing and conflicts. The first paragraph on page 12 concludes that "faith and prayer are really stronger than sin [worldliness], because Christ is stronger than Satan." The bottom of page 12 and the top of page 13 then ruminate upon a former Belstead student named Edith, and her sister Fanny, whose "evil" love of dancing, parties, and the theatre were encouraged by their "weak" parents. Fanny had died that autumn, and now apparently, Edith wondered "if Fanny would have done just as she did, had she known her end was near."

was influenced among other things by current ideas of child-raising, faith, and race. The historian's biases are inevitable.

Still, as scholars who study life-writing tell us, learning about an individual's struggles allow us self-reflection, even though we know that private records are not windows into "real" life.[46] Fact-finding also helps historians to recognize and analyze the thought processes of the recorder. Take, for example, the nineteen-year-old Constance's sincere "hope that

[her] long for excitement of feeling [would] pass away," yet the same entry bemoaned her "ignorance in love."[47] Her green book also omitted facts about her young adulthood. Her diary of 1871, for instance, briefly mentioned that she and Gabrielle stayed in "London for three months to take drawing lessons" which, to *us*, seems astonishing given Victorians' views on activities for the meeker sex.[48] We might surmise that whether biased, contradictory, or cursory, facts build vivid pictures of a past.

What about an anomalous fact? Is writing about an incident that does not tie back to a culture worthwhile? Is it a fact if we cannot authenticate it? The cultural historian Robert Darnton thinks so. Even if we cannot decipher the language in a text, it is a history in-of-itself that might unearth the origins of the individual's thought processes. Writing in the 1980s, Darnton's fascinating concept of what he called, "incident analysis," utilized methods adopted by anthropologists to garner knowledge about often-illiterate ancient cultures. His *Great Massacre ... in French Cultural History* (1984) did not explore the social upheaval from the French Revolution. Rather, his interest lay in uncovering the lived experiences of individuals before their insurgency. His curiosity about why an apprentice gleefully massacred his master's cat (and indeed many stray cats) led Darnton to surmise that the apprentice had not simply revolted against poor wages and living conditions in France. Cats symbolized sex and witchcraft; therefore, the apprentice's stringing up of cats outside the master's domicile also "shamed" the unfaithful wife. Far from senseless sadism, the cat massacre was an incident rich in symbolic critique about the behavior of those in power.[49]

As Darnton explored the possibilities of incident analysis, budding microhistorians carefully analyzed how minutia—words, comments, phrases, and so on—disclosed the particularity of a mindset. To notice the distinct, they argued, the microhistorian should first attain an in-depth knowledge of the larger culture and individual or event under observation.[50] In fact, years before I noticed Constance's anomalous remark written in 1871, I was intrigued by how asceticism had imbibed in her a curious reveling in pain,

> One day I [Constance] walked towards the field at the end of the garden and went very carefully in between the hazel bushes and kneeled on last year's dead leaves. When I got up, I looked down at my bare knees and I saw that some of the leaves were holly and that they clung on. I thought, "Holly prickles and I did not feel it. Oh, this was *real*, real prayer."[51]

Constance, aged ten, thought this "symbolic crucifixion of the flesh was proof of faith," and such self-seeking continued. At age twenty, she relished her mother's "Saying" from psalms 37.3.4: "God *gives*, but this does not mean He *grants* the desires of thy heart. *I* [Constance] think denial *is* more satisfactory than fulfillment!" As Mary King sardonically noted, Louisa chose "particular Sayings'" when each daughter entered womanhood, and psalms 37.3.4 did indeed shape Constance's emotional development. At age fifty-six, she still claimed that "faith [was] *NOT* about human gratification. It [was] about gaining 'Perfection' through self-denial!" What might we make of her abnegation? We cannot of course associate it with the sexologist Havelock Ellis's introduction of "female masochism" in 1897.[52] But we might propose that being raised on "religious despair" drove Constance to inculcate compensatory forms of suffering.[53] Even so, should we presume her acquiescence to self-denial? Not entirely, which returns us to her anomalous comment in 1871.

Although Constance could not befriend social equals, she explored intimacy apart from her mother's watchful eyes through "duty" or Bible study with Hawksworth villagers. On the one hand, her attempts to convert the pretty young Hetty Lawrence echoed middle-class female culture: "We are *just* like sisters," Hetty told Constance as the latter, despite their social inequality, "marvelled at Hetty's beauty, faith, and wisdom." Constance justified their friendship through faith: "We are equal in God's eyes."[54] However, in 1870 at age twenty-one, Constance confessed to physical desire for Hetty: "Should her [Hetty's] sweet smile prove more attractive than unity in Christ? Surely not, yet its beyond my control!"[55]

We have noted that Victorians adopted propriety about sex and Constance, likewise, did not explain her romantic, possibly sex feelings. Nonetheless, facts about these elusive female bonds have been established among historians. Smith-Rosenberg's "Female World" (1975) proposed "an alien" world by exploring letters between middle-class friends, among them "Molly" and "Helena." As Molly told Helena after one visit: "Imagine yourself kissed many times by one who loves you so dearly;" and to Helena's future husband: "Until you came along, I believe she loved me almost as girls love their lovers."[56] In similar fashion, Eliza Linn Linton swooned over "the most exquisite creature under heaven when [Adelaide] la[id] her long white arm along [Eliza's] shoulder!"[57] Historians after Smith-Rosenberg confirmed that honeyed words, sensual caresses, and long kisses on the lips between mother-daughter, sister, cousin, and friend co-existed with piety and heteronormativity.[58] So far, Constance's relations with Hetty aside from class seemed "normal" for the time.

Still, on the other hand, in 1871 Constance, aged twenty-two, began to define her romantic feelings for Hetty in a far more distinct way. After she began her daily diary, her green book evolved into a record about faith and sexual feeling. Her diary noted "fascinate[ion] with the new electrical experimentation of wire" at the Crystal Palace. Her green book, meanwhile, gave electricity a particular nature: "It is as if we [Hetty and Constance] both hold the end of electric chains! Thrills! Thrills! Beyond Control! Sparks exchange between us, only *I* know I am holding God."[59] Her new language of love seemed charged and more unusual. After all, beyond the science museum, late Victorians had little knowledge of electricity, for it was not yet even installed in homes. So, who or what influenced Constance? It remains unclear since she neither explained nor repeated her comment. We might assume that it was not familial based, given her mother's view of sentiment. In fact, Constance now "kept [her] green book strictly private."[60] Let us return to Robert Darnton's claim that historians may uncover words that seem antithetical to the past culture under study. Constance's feelings for Hetty seemed to counter ideas of women's "sexless naivety" and fervent descriptions of pious romantic friendship mentioned above. To date, no historians have cited late-Victorian women's use of electricity to characterize passionate same-sex feeling.

Darnton suggests that obtuse language, at best, may be situated indirectly within intersecting discourses.[61] So, if the term electric sparks seemed non-normative to female–female effusing, what about the idea of electricity itself? What did Victorians say about its invention in 1871? A search through both primary and secondary sources revealed virtually nothing written about electricity until the late 1870s, long after Constance had made her comment. Moreover, most publications focused on electricity as a technological and social breakthrough. The engineering press, for example, regaled readers with such "improvements" as reading without eyestrain and facial recognition. Other writing described how "strangers arriving in London by night [were] deeply impressed by the beauties of science!" There were a few naysayers as well: "Electricity is a great scientific achievement, but it is not the sort of thing that anyone wants."[62] Relations between light, environment, and bodily practice seemed central to the debates. In general, Victorians thought electric lighting was "more sanatory" than gas lighting. Gone was the "effluvia [and] blackened earth

[from] from aging gas pipes, [and] *light* allowed sight to function naturally."[63]

How did these comments relate to Constance's remark? They did not. We cannot situate her specific link of electricity with discourses of desire in late-Victorian culture. Her remark thus seems a history in-of-itself; a fact that was not *significantly* influenced by outside influences. If we hypothesize that Constance's description of sex feeling was unusual for her gender, we may "queer" her complex mindset. In this, the queer pioneer Judith Butler's dismantle of femininity and sex is notable, for she showcased how drag was "a signifying gesture through which gender itself is established." Her wish to establish gender as a social performance helped historians to conceive gender as among a series of identifications that individuals mediate over a lifetime.[64] Certainly, Victorian ideas of gender, class, sexuality, and nation led Constance to feel simultaneously empowered (elite) and disempowered (female). Yet her unusual religious upbringing meant that she did not "perform" desire as others of her class and gender.

When queer theorists tore down the binaries of male/female and gay/straight, they did so to illuminate "the queer" excluded from heteronormative divisions.[65] We will not however assign to Constance a queer identity, as that would be as presentist as her use of "mental damage" to describe her mid-Victorian past. "Queer" helps us to explain her paradoxical struggles as an elite ascetic who, denied female friendship, sought passion "undercover" with a female villager. We may consider Constance's experience of sex feeling with Hetty a part of Victorian culture, albeit one that lay beneath larger discourses of female sexuality. It seems possible that other Victorian women culled other discourses of same-sex desire if Victorians deemed women pure, sexless, or sexually naïve. What treasures or facts lie out there, still unknown?

In 1871, Constance tried to explain her sparks with Hetty as "a natural force" drawing her to God while effusing over Hetty's view of fleshy desire: "I [Hetty] *feel* the dark chains [of electric sparks], but I keep a piece of God unruffled in my heart."[66] Interestingly, her description of sparks as a natural force in 1871 predated the sexologist Havelock Ellis's depiction of "the unruly force of human nature" in 1897.[67] Nor did she explain dark chains or God's calming heart, which leaves readers to speculate whether one or both women thought desire was to be suppressed or was irrepressible. Was their conversation based upon Constance's distinct imagination of electricity with atonement-based proselytizing? Did they struggle to choose God over human love? Or did they willingly engage in a ritualistic mediation between desire and resistance? It remains unclear. Readers might understand Constance's wish to keep her feelings for Hetty a "secret" from her mother who curbed all emotional feelings. But why did Constance "hide [her subsequent] friendships from authority figures?"[68] Did she fear that her same-sex feelings went beyond feminine ideals or acceptable Evangelical conversion? This book shall reveal that these questions prove challenging to answer.

Constance's sense of self, formed during her childhood and young womanhood, shows how the atypical tells us more about the typical, and vice versa. She did not intend to buttress future studies on Victorian ideas of femininity, class, nation, religion, or sex, but her records have proved excellent sources for that. We better understand how one Victorian woman's sense of self was shaped by her family and culture, and that self-formation is also a fluid and multiple process. We might not understand Constance's awakening to dark chains or her attraction to the "beauty of a lifelong crucifixion." Yet such feelings fueled her need to connect to others, like Hetty, and more particularly, to garner her ascetic mother's approval. In 1869, she excitedly wrote: "Mother is slow to admit anyone to her 'circle,' but she now believes *me* to be a Christian!" Louisa's impact upon Constance's life was clear. The green book of 1871 laid out Edward Irving's schema for salvation: "We are under *complete* domination of three enemies, the flesh, the world, and Satan. Are we helpless? No, because God has left us Christ's Atonement, which is enough to employ us."[69] Mid-to-late-Victorian Evangelicals had long disused atonement thinking and terror as conversion and forms of self-denial, but Constance embraced it at Girton and Westfield.

Certainly, Constance Maynard's sense of religious despair is difficult to grasp. Yet even as the elderly Constance said, "Mother did me untold mental damage" she added, "but I see that I was beginning to find who I was through religious and intellectual inspiration."[70] Here, again, we glimpse aspects of Constance's self-formations that went beyond her society's ideas about gender, class, sex, nation, and faith. Her intimacy with Hetty forged her path of same-sex sexual self-exploration. For decades, she not only understood but acted upon her "irrepressible feelings." Yet at the same time, her need to suffer for human love *seemed* excruciating: "I hate self-denial!" she exclaimed at age fifty-six. "I would break it if I could!" Yet, apparently, "when [her] attempts at self-denial did not meet with the response from Heaven which [she] looked for, [she] adopted even more punitive measures."[71] Could we offer an alternative reading of Constance's thoughts? We might note that some early twentieth-century scientists challenged Havelock Ellis' notion of female masochism by typifying it as a form of female agency rather than "natural female meekness."[72] If we did, would it suggest that faith was, for Constance, both a public and private platform of power? After all, duty to her familial faith impelled her to forge an innovative women's college and try to evangelize the world. Perhaps her ascetic faith does raise new questions about Victorian femininity, sexuality, faith, and agency. Chapter 3 takes this up in exploring her sense as an Evangelical prophet.

Notes

1. *GB*, 20 February 1886, 142.
2. *A*, I, 1, "Childhood 1849–60," 7–11, written in January 1915.
3. Mary King, *Reminiscences of the Maynard Family, 1837–1901*, 30–31, Special Collections, Courtesy of Queen Mary University of London Archives/Constance Maynard/CLM. Reference CLM 6/3/1. Hereafter cited as King, *Reminiscences*, with page number. First names are used to distinguish family members in this and other chapters. Otherwise, Constance will be referred to as Maynard.
4. For politics and economics see Matthew, "Introduction," in Matthew ed., *The Nineteenth Century*, 1–38; and Heyck, *Intellectual Life*, 1–13.
5. Firth, *Constance Louisa Maynard*, 50–59. Louisa ne Hillyard's ancestors, the Tahourdins and d' Albaics, had in 1865 fled the family estates and come to England as Protestant refugees. The Reform Act (1832) gave propertied middle-class men voting rights.
6. *A*, I, 1, "Childhood 1849–60," 7–23, written in January 1915.
7. Ibid., 50–81; and Firth, *Constance Louisa Maynard*, 15–21.
8. See Hilton, *Age of Atonement*, 64; and Heyck, *Intellectual Life*, 44.
9. *D*, March 1871, 23.
10. *A*, I, 1, "Childhood 1849–60," 11–12, written in January 1915.
11. Ibid., 13.
12. See King *Reminiscenses*, 30; and Firth, *Constance Louisa Maynard*, 16.
13. Firth, *Constance Louisa Maynard*, 33–34.
14. See Davies, *Thoughts*, 33.
15. See *GB*, 1 January 1866, 1-2; for mid-Victorian cultural norms, see Gorham, *Victorian Girl*, 154–161; and for female education see Joyce Senders Pederson, "Schoolmistresses and Headmistresses: Elites and

Education in Nineteenth-Century England," *Journal of British Studies* 15 (1975), 137–143.
16. *A*, III, 8, "1871," 196, written in 1915. For female piety see, Callum Brown, *The Death of Christian Britain* (London: Routledge, 2001); and Bebbington, *Evangelicalism*, 75–105.
17. See Newsome, *Victorian World*, 158; and Heyck, *Intellectual Life*, 84–85.
18. *D*, February 1871, 12; and *GB*, 5 July 1871, 197.
19. See *GB*, 5 July 1871, 197. For more see Jane Garnett, "Religious and Intellectual Life," in *The Nineteenth Century*, ed., Colin Matthew, 215–217.
20. Cited in Hilton's *Atonement*, 286.
21. See *GB*, 13 March 1871, 23. For differences in Evangelical thinking see Bebbington, *Evangelicalism*, 22, 75–105.
22. *A*, I, II, "Childhood 1849–60," 3–28, written in January 1915; King *Reminiscences*, 5–6; and Firth, *Constance Louisa Maynard*, 12–15.
23. *GB*, 3 December 1869, 7; and Edward Irving, "On the Humanity of Christ," *The Morning Watch*, 1, (1829), 400–421. For societal response to Irving, see Hilton, *Age of Atonement*, 170–177.
24. In her *A*, I, 3, "Childhood 1849–60," 36, written in January 1915, Maynard noted, "Mother dissuaded all sentiment when we read from our Bible" as it prevented one from seeking divine grace.
25. King, *Reminiscences*, 30–31; and Firth, *Constance Louisa Maynard*, 30.
26. Compare Firth, *Constance Louisa Maynard*, 31, with *A*, I, 3, "Childhood 1849–60," 36, written in January 1915.
27. *GB*, 16 April 1866, 192.
28. *A*, I, 3, "Childhood 1849–60," 56, written in January 1915.
29. Firth, *Constance Louisa Maynard*, 38–42.
30. For Henry, see *D*, 4 May 1871, 2. For more on scientific thinking see Rose, *Psychological Complex*, 64–93; and Heyck, *Intellectual Life*, 190–195. The indigenous in the Eastern Cape colony comprised of a complex Xhosa assemblage of pastoral tribes. They proved a significant barrier to European expansion; the nine so-called wars were the most visible symbols of this confrontation. In terms of European conflict, when the Dutch Boers ceded the colony to the British in 1814, it was renamed the Cape of Good Hope and became English-speaking (Porter, *History of British Empire*, 84).
31. See *GB*, February 12, 1868, 69; *D*, 4 May 1871 2.
32. Bratlinger, *Dark Vanishing*, 169. For more on the scientist, Thomas Malthus, Poor Relief, and Darwin, see Newsome, *Victorian World Picture*, 16–18, 198–199; and Darnton, "Society and Economic Life," in *The Nineteenth Century*, ed., Colin Matthew, 71–75.

33. Maynard, *We Women*, 130. We will refer to race in this book as we understand it. Otherwise, we explain how others viewed the concept.
34. *D*, 3 July 1871, 23. Henry's opinion of the miners on strike at Laxey, the Lake District, reflected elite views of "idle pauperism" (see Newsome, *Victorian World Picture*, 15–25).
35. *GB*, 16 April 1871, 192.
36. See *GB*, 3 July 1871, 23; 26 March 1867, 52; and Firth, *Constance Louisa Maynard*, 16.
37. *A*, II, 4, "1865," 68, written in May 1915. Primogeniture was an ancient custom that dictated the right of succession of the business and estate belonged to the firstborn son.
38. *A*, 1, 3, "Adolescence 1863–64," 40–41, written in February 1915.
39. When bankruptcy hit the family, the single Gabrielle and Josephine moved to a small cottage to live a meagre life. Constance, unlike her unmarried sisters was self-sufficient as a pioneer female professional, but she could not forgive Harry's failure to adequately protect her sisters as an "elite head of family should" (*A*, III, 11, "1872," 338, written in May 1915).
40. See Weeks "Social Construction of Sexuality," 1–6; and John Maynard, *Victorian Discourses on Sexuality and Religion* (Cambridge: Cambridge University Press, 1993). For feminine norms see Gorham, *Victorian Girl*, 54–55, 91–96. For prescriptive literature of the time, see, for example, Edward Clarke, *Sex in Education* (Boston: James Osgood, 1873).
41. *A*, I, 2, "Adolescence 1861–62," 40, written in January 1915.
42. See Saunders, *About Women, Love and Marriage*, 162; Dinah Mulock Craik, *Thoughts about Women* (London: Hurst and Blacket, 1858), 48; Eliza Lynn Linton, *The Autobiography of Christopher Kirkland*, 3 vols. (London: Routledge and Sons, 1883); and Beatrice Webb, *My Apprenticeship* (London: Longman's Green, 1926).
43. *GB*, 7 February 1869, 107; and 19 February 1869, 112.
44. See *A*, I, 3, "Adolescence," 59–64, written in February 1915; and Firth, *Constance Louisa Maynard*, 44, 49.
45. Ludmilla Jordanova, *History in Practice 2nd ed.* (Bloomsbury Academic, 2010), 104, 161; and see also Richard Evans, *In Defence Of History*, (London: Granta Books, 1997), 115–126.
46. For life writing see, for example, Susan Ware "Writing Women's Lives: One Historians Perspective," *Journal of Interdisciplinary History*, 49, 3 (2012) 416; and Bella Brodzki and Celeste Schenck, *Life/Lines: Theorizing Women's Autobiography, Biography and Gender* (Oxford: Oxford University Press 1988).
47. *GB*, 7 February 1869, 107; 9 March 1869, 135; and 10 August 1869, 200.
48. See, *D*, March 1871, 23; 23 July 1871, 65; and September 1872, 45.

49. Robert Darnton, *The Great Massacre and Other Episodes in French Cultural History* (New York: Vintage Books, 1984).
50. For microhistory, see, for example, Richard D. Brown, *Self-Evident Truths: Contesting Equal Rights from the Revolution to the Civil War* (New Haven CT: Yale University Press, 2017); and Ginzburg, "Microhistory: Two or Three Things," 10–35.
51. Quote taken from psalms 37.3.4 (Firth, *Constance Louisa Maynard*, 27). See Hilton, *Age of Atonement*, 286, which claims that atonement-thinking prompted individuals to engage in self-torment and to fear God.
52. See *GB*, 19 February 1869, 107, 6 March, 1905, 34; King, *Reminiscences*, 32; and for Ellis' work and societal reaction to it see Porter and Hall, *Facts of Life*.
53. For more on girls' suffering under their mother's asceticism, see for example, John Stachniecoski, *Prosecutory Imagination: English Puritanism and Literature of Religious Despair*, (Oxford: Oxford University Press, 1991), 50–61, who investigates the impact of religious despair on individuals.
54. *GB*, 28 November 1868, 46.
55. *GB*, 8 October 1870, 287.
56. See Smith-Rosenberg, "Female World," 1–2, 7–9; Rich, "Compulsory Heterosexuality," 631–790; and Faderman, *Surpassing Love of Men*.
57. Linton, *Autobiography of Christopher Kirkland*, 181.
   See for example, Lilian Wald, "Smashing; Women's Relationships Before the Fall," *Chrysalis* 8 (1979), 17–27; Leila J. Rupp, "Imagine My Surprise: Women's Relationships in Historical Perspective." *Frontiers* 5 (1980), 61–70; and Lisa Moore, "'Something More Tender Still Than Friendship': Romantic Friendship in Early-Nineteenth-Century England," *Feminist Studies* 18, 1 (2009): 499–521.
58. Compare *D*, 16 March 1871, 23, with *GB*, 28 March 1871, 13.
59. *A*, II, 4, "Adolescence 1866–71," 59, written in April 1925.
60. For more on Darnton and language see Tosh ed., *Historians On History*, 315.
61. Paget Higgs, *The Electric Light, and Its Practical Applications* (London: 1879), 6; and "Electric Lighting for the City of London,' *Electrician* 6 (April 1881), 246.
62. Christopher Otter, "Cleansing and Clarifying: Technology and perception in Nineteenth-Century London," *Journal of British Studies*, 43, (2004), 55–57.
63. Butler, *Gender Trouble*, x–xxi.
64. For a good account of the development of queer theory see Beasley, *Gender & Sexuality*, 161–165; and A. Jagose, *Queer Theory: An Introduction* (New York: New York University Press, 1996).
65. *GB*, 21 March 1871, 138.

66. For more on Ellis, see Beasley, *Gender & Sexuality*, 138–139.
67. *A*, III, 11, 368, written in 1915.
68. Compare *GB*, 6 September 1869, 88, with Irving, who wrote: "Christ's 'sinful substance' was not inherently holy, otherwise, the Atonement would have been void" (Bebbington, *Evangelicalism*, 93).
69. *A*, II, 4, "Adolescence 1865–66," 59, written in April 1925.
70. *GB*, June 1905, 88–90.
71. For female masochism, see Alison Moore, "Rethinking Gendered Perversion and Degeneration in Visions of Sadism and Masochism, 1886–1930," *Journal of the History of Sexuality*, 18, 1 (2009), 138.

CHAPTER 3

Evangelical Prophet at Girton, 1872–1875

Abstract Maynard's experiences at the innovative Girton College for women (1872–1875) provide novel insights into both society's crisis of faith and the culture of female friendship. The author first discusses how Maynard's unique study of the human mind or psyche not only implanted in her a lifelong conflict between science and self-determination, and faith and self-denial. Her sense as Evangelical prophet, which created a science–faith division at Girton, suggested that late Victorians were more agnostic than historians argue. Chapter 3 then questions historiography on female friendship in showcasing Maynard's aggressive coax of Girtonian love, Amy Mantle, to embrace yet resist their physical passion for God. The pious Maynard's actions not only implied her challenge of Victorians' idea of female submissiveness. As the author also notes, Maynard's intimacy with Mantle is one that historians avoid writing about: women who dominated women using pain. The author tackles this sensitive topic by highlighting *Maynard's* perception of how she treated Mantle, and why it influenced her future college bonds.

Keywords The Psyche • Evangelicalism • Roleplaying • Mentalité • Female Sexuality

In 1902, Maynard aged fifty-three bemoaned her failure as an Evangelical prophet:

> It really is sad that I [Maynard] can not make the world of good people see the extreme importance of this crisis of thought and belief! I can't, yet those who do come say it [Bible] throws floods of light, that the OT [Old Testament] stories are all given back, and that hope and new life and impetus spring up everywhere ... [We] lament careless Agnosticism.[1]

Her lament about careless agnostics had a long history, for God first "Called her" in 1868 at age fourteen. She had read "Isaiah 6 and was struck by, 'Whom shall I send?' [She had] thought, 'a real prophet is needed to fight worldliness, now, as ever it was in Isaiah's time.'" Her rumination, of course, relayed that of an adolescent raised to "shun the world and bring 'Will' to humble spirit."[2] Yet her *longing* as a prophet invoked self-determination. After all, during childhood, she had opposed ascetic home life through make-believe. At age twenty-two (1871), she explored electric sparks with Hetty Lawrence. In 1872, when "life took a dramatic turn," her agency was as clear. She learned of the cause and convinced her parents to enroll her at Girton, the first women's college in Cambridge founded by Emily Davies in 1869.[3] This chapter explores two incidents caused by Maynard in 1875 that seem bizarre but were not incongruous for the time. First, was Maynard's arrogant Biblicism that tore Girton apart, yet her actions resembled Victorians' crisis of faith. Second, was Maynard's discomfort over her ardent conversion of Girton love Amy Mantle. Their relations, while a part of female culture, seemed astonishing in predicting what became the stigmatization of female-female passion in the mid-1920s.[4]

When the older Maynard reviewed her Girton experiences in her autobiography, she recalled the words of the prophet Isaiah who said,

> "The mountains and fields shall break before you in singing," and most surely these words were true for me [Maynard]. Of course, there was winter, which was barren, but spring offered us hesitating beauties that expanded, week by week, until we could walk through copses to spaces like heavens, upbreaking through the earth.[5]

Her metaphorical passage characterized how "Girtonians' walk through [male] copses" forged women's rights to higher learning but that there were huge drawbacks. They sat the same Tripos or degree exams as men, but Cambridge deemed them "women's examinations" until 1948.[6] As a result, Maynard initiated in 1882 the London-based Westfield to gain women new access to university degrees. Her reference to "hesitating beauties" meanwhile, hinted at love, whilst "spaces like heavens" relayed her life-long dedication to fight agnosticism as God's prophet.[7] In essence, the autobiography reflected Maynard's three transformations at Girton (1872–1875) that were outlined in her diaries. First was her new-found enthusiasm for science. The six pioneering students among them Louisa Lumsden, Sarah Woodhead, and Rachel Cook had initiated activities typical to men's institutions: use of surnames; study circles; and a Debating Society. At first, Maynard "found the academic pace and living conditions inhuman." Her diary further explained,

> College is overfilled and so, I stay in a large unheated shed called the iron room on Girton's grounds. It is too hot in the summer and too cold in the winter. The library in the main college is also the lecture room and the common room. The dining room, a dark, dank basement room, with barred windows and repellant food, seems more like a prison.[8]

However, although Girton seemed bleak, and she "often fell asleep stiff with cold, [she] awaken[ed] each morning with *anticipation* for classes!" There were subjects for the "Little-Go" first-year examination such as Latin, Euclid, Arithmetic, and William Paley's *Evidences of the … Deity* (1794); a required reading at Cambridge alongside Darwin. At the end of their second-year students "sat the Additionals" in algebra, trigonometry, and mechanics (physics). Then came the Tripos in third year in either the Classics or Natural Sciences. In the meantime, "the weekly swim at the public pool [was] as much an experience for ladies … as evening wrestling in the library." We also discover what Girton Mistress Emily Davies proclaimed were the capabilities of women. The diary continued:

> One [Sarah Woodhead] gained the honour of senior Optime for Mathematics, and another [Rachel Cook] beat the three best men in Classics. This is a double triumph in face of the verdict that as women, they were sure to fail! Our first two out of the thicket [with Tripos] are not placed [on the official university list]; but it was heartening to hear "three cheers for the Ladies" [at Convocation].[9]

When a determined Maynard persuaded her parents "to let her take the gold [Tripos]" after her first term at Girton, she carved a new trail. Her interest in Logic and Ethics led her to become the first Girtonian and, indeed, among the first Victorians to study the new Mental and Moral Sciences Tripos.[10] This Tripos gave women more of an equal opportunity with men since neither had studied human behavior previously. The subjects of Philosophy that investigated consciousness and that beyond objective experience were the "Mental" papers. The "Moral" papers, meanwhile, incorporated Logic and Ethics through such works as Adam Smith's *Wealth of Nations* (1776). This may seem odd, but as noted, *Wealth* considered links between economics, social organization, and the "character" of people. For her part, Maynard was likely "drawn to Logic" due to her ascetic upbringing.[11] At Girton, she had an affinity for Joesph Butler's sermons on "evil" hedonism as much as Immanuel Kant's *Critique of Pure Reason* (1781, 1787).[12]

Maynard eagerly recalled the outcome of her first transformation: "I learned how to weigh evidence and see the far-reaching value of principles ... It felt liberating! It was a special time. A new form of collective conscious left us shouting to be heard!"[13] She was not quite as certain of this at the time. Her diary condemned Girton's salute to human progress through Darwin's *On the Origin*; a work that she attributed to Victorian religious doubt. She was equally angry that "Mental Philosophy plunged [her] into thought that Will [human thought] was *agency*, not evil [as she had been raised to believe]."[14] She translated pages from Aristotle and wrote copious notes on eighteenth-century philosophers like Kant, Jeremy Bentham, and John Lock, before she tackled the Victorian thinkers John Stuart Mill, Herbert Spencer, and Alexander Bain.

The diary briefly noted philosophers of interest. Of all "moral" theorists, Maynard was drawn to Immanuel Kant: "I like his idea of rational thought that has no goals." Her opinion of "mental" writers differed: "[John] Locke is unfathomable, but I'm intrigued by his [notion] of consciousness beyond outside rule ... Read [John] Stuart Mill's epoch making *System of Logic*! Was marvelous! ... But dislike Bain's materialist *Senses* as well as Spencer's survival of fittest, that shews how we adapt to circumstances." However, of all thinkers, she loathed the Utilitarian philosopher Jeremy Bentham and his "chilly religion. *He* [Bentham] says, 'we obey only to *earthly* rules, rather than to religious conviction. *We* create our own beliefs and act upon them!'" In Bentham's view, people's experience with joy and pain led them to act in ways that increased their happiness. Maynard likely hated Bentham's implication that *she* chose to seek pain. Far from feeling liberated by Girton's milieu, she called it "Satan's seat!"[15]

Maynard, as we recall, had encountered the challenge of science in adolescence. Her parents had tried to link Darwin's ideas with new Christian-biological work that formulated evolutionary cycles with Biblical creation.

She thus deftly "feigned" enthusiasm for *On the Origin* at Girton to avoid conflict with agnostic peers Rachel Cook and Louisa Lumsden. In private, she discussed Christian science with a Cambridge clergyman who said: "Think of evolution as a force of God that gives *you* opportunity to discern good over evil." His words did not help, and again, in this she was not unusual. By the mid-1870s, Anglican ministers no longer preached that Christian science reinforced God's presence in the world while, Evangelicals, in general, now deemed it "bad science." Some clergymen disentangled science from faith through Christology or personal knowledge of Christ. As Maynard told Lumsden: "Just as rays of light are refracted by the material of the lens, so Christ is refracted by God's light."[16] She could neither ignore science nor detach it from faith.

THE EMERGING EVANGELICAL PROPHET

As scientific theories plagued Maynard, they inevitably forged her second profound transformation. This moment happened at Girton on a Sunday in November 1872:

> College etiquette required we mingle, but it was the Sabbath and I longed to turn the conversation to Christ but dared not suggest it ... But one day, as I sat there listening to debate on some new novel, I suddenly thought, "God has chosen me out of thousands of English girls to hold the most difficult post in the world."[17]

God wished her to combat religious doubt "by sending out devout university-trained women to evangelize the world." Maynard was not alone in feeling "Called;" historians have noted many over time who felt chosen to save a society that eschewed faith.[18] Our opening quote relayed Maynard's deep fret over the crisis of agnosticism in 1902. In 1872, as a prophet at Satan's seat, she felt hopeful, even though it "was a lonely post. [She] begged the beautiful Rachel Cook to accept the Bible, as it would benefit [Cook's] life and aims." She hoped to convert Louisa Lumsden "who was much admired, but [Lumsden] too, was unsparing in scorn of the Bible." Starved for Christian companionship, Maynard crossed social barriers to sit with local lower-middle-class tailors on Sundays. In the meantime, she diligently prepared herself for her difficult post. She passed her Little-Go and Additionals with a First Class in December 1873 and June 1874, respectively. She gained her Tripos in the Mental and Moral Sciences in 1875 (Fig. 3.1).[19]

Fig. 3.1 (Left) Groups of early Hitchin students, ca. 1870. Louisa Lumsden is seated to the far right and Rachel Cook is seated next to her, with pioneers Emily Townsend, Isabel Gibson, and Anna Lloyd standing behind them. Lumsden and Cook were among the first women to complete studies in the Classics. Courtesy of St. Leonards School Archives, St. Andrews. (Right) Groups of early Hitchin students, ca. 1873. Amy Mantle, who would form a relationship with Maynard at Girton in 1874, is standing in the middle of the back row. Courtesy of St. Leonards School Archives, St. Andrews.

Maynard's green book also invoked a third transformation that conflicted with her second one. In June 1873 she wrote: "I feel that Girton has given me 'a good shaking'—some things I considered 'fixed' are now left more open and have raised questions. All that was 'true and real' only stands the firmer,

> and yet I cannot dismiss that Girton tempts me to be filled with indescribable longings to do, or be, or feel something different—wider, fuller! These feelings seem unworthy when I think of God who has stored my life. The basis of my belief and action are not as strong as I suppose. I cannot bring *every* thought to God. There is silence between us."[20]

She now confessed that Darwin and Bain "gave [her] innovative ideas and insights." She also engaged in what her mother would call "foolish sentiment" in admiration for Cook and Lumsden, whose "strong assertive secularism disarmed [her] again and again."[21] Her family heard about college life, particularly the advantages of Girton's move in 1873 to a location closer to Cambridge. Students could more easily attend lectures and meet other pioneer female students from Merton and Newnham Halls. She also regaled her family with "amusing tales about the silly cartoons in *Punch Magazine* that mocked college women," or the time when a male Cambridge student "asked the maid, 'What's the point [of Girton]?' and she primly answered, 'Tis for *educational* purposes, Sir.'"[22] However, her Tripos was another matter. She avoided discussing them with her family and felt uncomfortable about it. Her studies, she realized, had become a means to escape Oakfield.

This noted, homelife during vacations still influenced Maynard. Her mother repeatedly pressed her about "duty to faith," and she fretted over her failure to convert peers:

> They [Girtonians] all think that human nature is radically good, and that it can follow out and embody the highest ideal, if it chooses to make the effort ... One tells me that she is quite good within and has no need of the "horrors of the Cross" to save her soul; if she makes a mistake, she is sorry for it, but the total motives that hold sway are all good. Another tells me that the Evangelical outlook is all illusion, a childish sort of illusion too.[23]

Because Evangelicals were known to follow life-principles based upon Biblicism, Crucifixiation, and active conversion, they were now incorrectly deemed intellectually lacking.[24] Maynard faced similar criticism at Girton, but it worsened over her final year that began in October 1874. On the one hand, she enjoyed her status as "Senior Student (SS)." Davies consulted her on college matters and placed her in charge of sports; indeed, the idea of leadership over twenty-two students excited her. On the other hand, the "new batch" of Girtonians created a troubling dynamic. The younger students such as Amy Mantle respected her as S.S., but the talented older genteel Malvena Borchhardt, and Henrietta Muller, seemed impertinent. They knew she had standing, and was pious, yet they coaxed Girtonians towards nonreligious views through "free thought," a new philosophical viewpoint allied with secularism and atheism. In Borchardt's and Muller's radical-minded view, the Bible was not Infallible, as Christians claimed: "It was a fake, a story told by men that was mired in dogmatism."[25]

We examined Maynard's dissonant voices about faith during her childhood, but her "crisis of faith" at Girton relayed far deeper anxiety. In 1873 she had remarked: "I have thrown myself into worldly amusements with a fondness I have not felt before. Yet the pleasure of life here [Girton] depends a *lot* on one's feelings and study, *doesn't* it?" A year later, she "worried over 'dropping' [her] position. Outwardly, [she] had become much more like them [the agnostic Louisa Lumsden and Rachel Cook]."[26] By early 1875, however, she was frantic:

> I have lost my faith *entirely*! Surely, it *cannot* be! The natural sciences seem to me to be strong in deism; belief in the existence of a creator, but not one involved with us or the world. I could see their [free thought] side. I want to believe in it [Bible] as the ground of redemption, but I cannot see any link between science and faith.[27]

Thomas Huxley had coined agnosticism in 1869 to characterize the new phenomenon of religious doubt. Agnosticism was not, however, as dire as Maynard's verge on atheism. Her suspicion that "the Bible was a bigoted man's book" echoed that of Borchardt and Muller. Desperate, and confused, Maynard was rescued through what her cousin Mary King called, "red hot evangelizing." Her much-adored brother Harry had newfound admiration for the gifted American evangelists, Moody, and Sankey, who aimed "to revive London through a huge campaign."[28] When Maynard attended their sermon at the Agricultural Hall in April 1875, she "felt *so* overwhelmed by the thousands that stood as if they really wished to be saved, that [she] returned to Girton [for the May Term of 1875] with a longing over the souls of others."[29]

"An Odd Disciple of Sorts"

Maynard's crisis of faith certainly emulated late-Victorian disarray over scientific thinking. But if we focus solely on how her struggles echoed the whole, we will miss the opportunity to provide new information about Victorian religious doubt. When we turn to the minutia (Girton), we discover a milieu embroiled in power struggles unusual to women. Girtonians had gained confidence as students (and women) and as a result, were more competitive with each other through activities such as debates. However, Maynard's vie for power was driven by her resolve to destroy free thought secularism. The idea of a theological discussion circle was first raised at Girton in early 1874. The proposal was vetoed, though Henrietta Muller's "lofty comment, 'Free rational thought could *well* test religion,'" had inflamed Maynard: "The unbelievers will *not* have their own way!"[30] She had initiated a Bible study group that had since gained her notoriety as a religious leader. Nonetheless, "red-hot evangelizing" impelled her aggressive block of Muller's and Borchhardt's control: "It took courage, and above all, patience," but by May eight (one-third) Girtonians attended her Bible study. Maynard aimed "to salve religious doubt ... and truly believe[d] that students bec[ame] close in a way otherwise impossible." Still, her overarching comment was telling: "No-one says more than yes, but they like to listen."[31] Her sense of purpose through Biblicism reaffirmed her role as an Evangelical prophet.

Biblical passages from Luke 12:32 conveyed Maynard's mission: "Fear not, little flock, for it is your Fathers good pleasure to give you the Kingdom." She would lead Girtonians to God despite opposition from free thought. Her "little flock devoured [her] with kisses and tender ministries and treated [her] as the final appeal in matters of the soul." Even so, most Girtonians thought her "an odd disciple of sorts," and the free thought mocked her little flock's attempts at conversion:

> One on their [free thought] side made them laugh with her account of Lizzie's midnight call and prayer beside her bed. She said she pretended to be converted. She even got Lizzie to pray in Muller's room, and our "weak Biblicism" and arguments over the Bible became a joke until they left college. The friction was intense.[32]

Sadly, these conflicts destroyed Girton's corporate and intellectual aim: unity against gender inequality through higher learning.

In June 1875, the bitterness between the camps peaked with devastating results. In general, Girtonians dreaded the eager proselytizers' "knock on their door to preach about sin and damnation." But the commotion caused by temper tantrums distracted students from their studies. When Muller sarcastically requested "a corridor between the camps" Maynard sadly confessed: "College is divided in two! It is all *my* doing. I have made a terrible mistake."[33] However, the way that she confronted her mistake is worth consideration. Her green book justified her decision to tell tutors: "We [Bible study members] *won't* attend debates because of 'controversial' topics like, 'is flirting wrong.'" Her autobiography condoned her behavior: "I *knew* that I could not go back."[34] At the time, free thought attacked her "deficiency of spirit" by ridiculing her belief in "everlasting retribution" for Adam's sin. They had a point. Atonement-thinking morally challenged the popularized incarnational-based, Rest in Faith. Nonetheless, Victorians regarded any scorn of faith sacrilegious, and Maynard was furious about it. Still, as the autobiography hotly defended her actions, the green book was not so sure: "I *envy* their [free thought] brilliance;" and again, "I am *ashamed* to be affiliated with ignorant students [little flock]."[35] Jealousy had not only contributed to disjuncture at Girton. Humiliation, it seems, drove Maynard to renegue on worldly activities to save face.

Maynard's reactions to Girton's split relayed conscious and unconscious thought processes. The green book invoked conflicted feelings: piety (duty to God through conversion); self-importance (righteousness and power through her role); self-doubt (uncertainty and shame over her mistakes); and jealousy yet frustration over free thought. Ultimately, however, the elderly Maynard deemed her actions wrong: "I cared more about my religious ambitions than [Girtonians] themselves."[36] Even so, her overall worry about Christianity was a part of the larger crisis in faith. This was evident, for example, in the clergy's increased struggle to define faith apart from secularist culture, and the dramatic rise in Sunday School attendance. What of Girton as an entity? May we consider its religious-secularist dynamic a fraction of the whole? According to Maynard, of the twenty-five enrolled, eight were Bible study members, six had joined free thought, while the remaining eleven "were undeclared."[37] The minutia suggested that intellectual Victorians (at least) were largely undecided on matters of faith and science. Is this important? We would need more evidence, of course, but our statistics have potential. Historians have recently challenged accounts of the era as one of increased doubt because such findings were based upon the census in 1851. They argue that other sources, such as newspapers and church records, conveyed that society remained religious regardless of science.[38] However, we might propose that while late Victorians clung to faith, they were more ambivalent about it than is argued.

Maynard's account of her Girton experiences also conveys microhistorians' idea of normal exception. Girtonians' study of "male" subjects helps us to conceive why women's higher learning dramatically altered notions of female capabilities. Meanwhile, Maynard's crisis of faith at Girton, while not extraordinary to the era, relays its nuances (at least for college women); for example, Maynard's religious power is exampled by her concept, "my little flock."[39] Certainly, women had few social rights and Victorians designated them meek, pious, and subservient in contrast to more aggressive ambitious men. Girton was deliberately located in a village outside Cambridge, and Emily Davies warned students "to convince society that [they] were *entirely fe*minine in manner."[40] But it seems that when given similar opportunities to men, Girtonians *were* aggressive and ambitious. Maynard felt it her religious duty to convert peers, yet she (and free thought) had few qualms in battles for power, even if it severed a college established upon the idea of female unity and corporatism.

Whether competitive, or religious, Girton's split clarifies the unique battles that pioneer college women faced. Their lack of secondary education in Classics and science meant that Girtonians' struggled with "unfathomable" lecturers who were "shunted" or replaced with private tutors. We may wonder at their success with examinations.[41] However, the fight between believers and non-believers was clearly destructive. For her part, Maynard nearly failed Mental Philosophy and felt disappointed by her "Second" in her Tripos after her distinctions in the Little-go and Additionals. Nonetheless, she managed to pass her exams and felt guilt-ridden about her little flocks' wasted hours on futile conversion. Many failed their Little-go and Additionals and left Girton without completing their studies. Some may have dropped out of Girton, anyway, but Maynard would ensure that Westfield students kept strictly to the curriculums required for degrees without distractions. She also initiated Sunday "Function;" the one day set aside to discuss theological matters and missionary and allied topics. Even so, Westfield students were neither pressured to attend Function nor expected to become missionaries.[42] Maynard had learned from her mistakes at Girton.

Mentalité, Female Sexuality, and Ardent Conversion

Maynard's variable accounts of her Girton experiences offer a past that she perhaps never intended. Historians certainly relish them, not only for their insights about women's higher learning. Maynard's memoirs notable windows into the worldview of her era. This interest in what French historians call, the mentalité, or spirit of the age, owed its important roots to a major revolution in the historical profession in place by the mid-twentieth century. Traditional political history toppled under the influential Annales School founded in 1929 by French historians Lucien Febvre and Marc Block, and well established by the 1950s. Annalists used quantification to measure a "total history" about ordinary people through inquiries into phenomena like social groups, cultural norms, climate, agriculture, commerce, and technology to gain a sense of the thinking of the age.[43] The Annales strongly influenced the new social history of the 1960s, and the ensuing fields of women's history, history of sexuality, and the genre of microhistory.

Women's history that emerged during second-wave feminism tended to showcase figures who challenged their society's negative mentalité about women. The idea that male–female relations reflected the thinking of an era was in turn, advanced by Joan Wallach Scott's use of "gender as a tool of analysis."[44] The development of historical fields often galvanized a flurry of interpretations on a topic. For example, following Smith-Rosenberg's "Female World" that explored the multiplicity of intimacy among nineteenth-century women, scholars like Leila Rupp and Martha Vicinus debated over whether the term "lesbian" was helpful to explain the possibly sexual depths of Victorian female friendship.[45] Such discussion invoked the history of sexuality that was inspired by the 1960s gay rights movement. The field had flourished following historians like Michel Foucault whose work exemplified the possibilities of studying sex. His *History of Sexuality* (1985) dismantled the metanarrative about "Victorians silence about sex" by showing how "excessive" literature about sex that while repressive, relayed much talk about sex even though Victorians deemed it private.[46]

We hypothesized that Maynard's ardor for Hetty Lawrence relayed new information about Victorian female sexuality and so, following Foucault, we might (again) wonder if other unusual writing about female–female desire exists. Our query recalls the microhistory movement that introduced an alternative historical method to that of traditional political history. Pioneer microhistorians' study of minutia warned historians about the dangers of generic accounts about "women" or "society;" we mentioned that Natalie Zemon Davis's *Return of Martin Guerre* (1983) utilized transcripts from a single trial about imposter-ship to exemplify how early modern France judged "proof."[47] Above, we speculated that the minutia (Girton college split) provided new insight into the mentalité of late-Victorian religious doubt. We also learned that writing on the thought processes of an era is never complete.

What about the influence of science on Maynard's mentalité? This may seem an odd question, but she was after all a pioneer student of human thinking. Earlier, we surmised that her sense of religious "duty" at Girton—heightened by visits home—led Maynard to avoid writing about her Tripos. Moreover, throughout her life, she insisted that God guided her actions, and as we recall, my biography proposed that faith caused trauma for both Maynard and her college loves.[48] But was this a narrow reading? What about her third transformation at Girton? Let us revisit her green book confession: "Girton has filled me with indescribable longings ... I cannot bring *every* thought to God." Her concluding thought was curious: "To *love*, is *not* like love of God! The heart recognizes, '*we* belong to each other!'"[49] She had, to that point, declared that love feeling was evil. Now, her view of love as a part of human nature echoed the mentalité of her time. Something had changed.

With the above in mind, I carefully re-examined Maynard's diaries and autobiography and happily discovered an overview of her Tripos, written in 1918 at age sixty-nine:

> I felt it [Tripos] was all rather bad, leading me to analyze, and doubt, and argue. Mental Philosophy burdened me with questions on feeling, perception, and sensory experience. I wrote stronger Tripos on moral conduct rather than pure thought ... I was led by [Immanuel] Kant's series of steps "I am, I ought, I will." But there is in me an unanalyzable point that is not subject to the theories of the rational or phenomena. I choose God.[50]

Maynard's passage echoed her angry green book entry in 1872: "Mental Philosophy plunges me into thought that Will [self-determination] is *agency*, not evil."[51] Yet we cannot ignore her claim to be "led by Kant's 'series of steps'" towards logical thought. We should also explore her interest in the ideas of earlier mentioned philosophers John Stuart Mill, Alexander Bain, and John Locke.

John Stuart Mill's *Autobiography* (1874) is first worth mentioning in relation to Immanuel Kant and Maynard's ascetic upbringing. Mill sadly told readers that his father's obsession with "the evil of self-conceit" shattered his self-esteem and led him to deem most feelings and actions "wrong." His father's view of conduct echoed Immanuel Kant's theory of logic: without reason, one succumbed to passions like lust or envy and would not be free. From Mill, we better understand why Kant's steps towards "morality" resonated with Maynard.[52] Yet, at Girton, she had called Mill's *System of Logic* (1843) "epoch making." The older Mill had in *System* refuted his father's "truths" of the mind by drawing upon natural science principles to speculate about human volition (rather than moral conduct).[53] Among his many followers was Alexander Bain, who in *Senses and the Intellect* (1855) reasoned that people conceived of feelings as *theirs* rather than actions to repress. For Bain, learning occurred through spontaneity, and we mentioned that he "gave [Maynard] innovative ideas and insights."[54] His view of knowledge building as gained through various pleasurable/painful experiences relayed that of John Locke, whose "concept of consciousness beyond outside rule" intrigued Maynard.

The elderly Maynard claimed to feel burdened by Mental Philosophy. Yet both the diary and green book implied that to a certain extent it freed her sense of self. The Mental Philosophers to whom she was drawn in the mid-1870s did not mention "psychology" (that only emerged as a discipline in 1904). But historians including Roger Smith and E.D. Baker propose that scientists like Locke, Mill, and Bain exhorted individual capacities in multiple ways through linking ideas to feeling and action.[55] Thus, perhaps inevitability, Maynard's belief systems were challenged by her Tripos. Her pursuit of physical intimacy with Girton peer Amy Mantle seems remarkable, given ideals of femininity and her ascetic faith; but science facilitated Maynard's exploration of "feelings" as *hers*, rather than actions to repress for faith.

Maynard did not explicitly describe having sex with Mantle. But we are nonetheless fortunate to have her frank account of female–female desire. Unfortunately, Mantle did not leave records behind, yet according to Maynard, she had no qualms about their passionate bond. What intrigues, however, is Maynard's discomfort over their relations not only as a pioneer of what we might call freedom of self-expression, but at a time when passion among women was deemed a part of female development. What we do know and cannot be fully surprised by is Maynard's initial horror upon first listening to Girtonians gush over female friends. While her peers were raised to engage in passionate female ties, she understood longings for Hetty Lawrence through a God who reproved human nature. She could not fully accept Girtonians' social upbringing at parties or attending the theatre. She certainly enjoyed "worldly activities" at Girton like singing and charades, but felt somewhat uncomfortable about it.[56]

Apparently, a few close college friends referred to each other as man or wife. This aspect of Girton bonds (perhaps typical to other women's colleges) distinguished them from mainstream female friendships steeped in heteronormativity with its assumptions of gender roles and heterosexuality. Maynard did not explain husband-wife roleplaying at Girton, except to imply that it involved some masculine and feminine "attributes." The "husband" held dominance while the "wife" was more deferent and "agreeable." There was, however, a negotiation of power, whereby debates on studies were conducted on an equal basis. Sometimes rings were exchanged and promises of fidelity made. For most Girtonians, however, husband-wife roleplaying did not interfere with the usual activities of heterosexual romance or marrying men after college.[57]

Most Girtonians considered Maynard a "cold, stern, and odd" woman because of her asceticism. After all, she "relish[ed] the idea of a lifelong crucifixion" and had debated "dark chains" of desire with Lawrence.[58] We might thus expect notions of torment that allured her would become a part of her college bonds. This is not to criticize Maynard, except to note the inconsistencies between her unusual faith-based mentalité and pioneer studies in human thought and agency. We speculated upon the young Maynard's penchant for suffering. Her admission at Girton, "*love*, is *not* like love of God," invoked a conflict, perhaps inspired by her enjoyment of self-denial.[59] But how might we analyze her complex mindset and longings? In the Introduction, we noted that historians of sexuality tend to avoid studying women who dominated women and we may do likewise.[60] Yet Maynard's (probably unintended) toy of Amy Mantle became an important part of her experiences with college loves. If we unpack the idea of power or dismantle what queer scholars call the "fixed" binary of domination/submission, we may find some solutions.[61] History happens when we ask different questions and revise former interpretations of the past (Fig. 3.2).

The twenty-three-year-old Maynard's bond with the orphaned but wealthy nineteen-year-old Mantle that began in March 1874 was possibly both women's first physical exploration of passion. Maynard was attracted to Mantle who was an enthusiastic Bible Study member because she was pretty, delicate, and purportedly genteel. When she fell in love with Mantle, Maynard turned to the philosopher-theologian William Paley's *Evidences* "to confirm God's acceptance of [her] feelings." She concluded: "He [Paley] shews that we *know* God, in part through our own nature. It is not simply knowing God; it is knowing the true estimate of *us*!"

Evidences was known at Cambridge as a solid work based upon historical evidence and, apparently, it gelled with Maynard's Tripos: "Amy [Mantle] *does need* to kiss me [Maynard]! Her lips bespeak of passionate loving that sends an irresistible appeal to my heart. *All* my reason gives way!" Kissing and fondling Mantle led to God, whereby "she would resist the human flame."[62]

We might ponder the hypocrisy of Maynard's proselytizing, but we should consider her social context. For example, scholars including Angharad Eyre explain that young Victorian missionaries bemoaned their

Fig. 3.2 Constance Maynard at Girton with fellow members of the Girton Bible meeting, ca. 1874. Maynard is seated on the left-hand side with her arm around Amy Mantle. Courtesy of Queen Mary University of London Archives/Westfield College/WFD. Reference WFD/25/ 1/1/1.

"stupid heart" when they chose human passion (female friendship) over God.[63] Did Maynard's intimacy with Mantle then, represent aspects of mainstream femininity? Not entirely, which returns us to her studies in Mental Philosophy: "Electric sparks from [Mantle's] loving disposition" inspired Maynard to explore passion through the unique Girton husband-wife roleplaying: "She [Mantle] wants me as husband to say *my* part of the wedding vows." Their subversive mother-daughter roleplaying further conveyed Maynard's relinquishing of feeling as evil: "When she [Mantle] comes 'to be loved,' often I call her baby, but *this* time, she leaned back full against me, and whispered, *Mother*, come to me!"[64]

Perhaps other Girtonians transitioned between husband and mother roleplaying. Yet such shifts in what Maynard called, "love," surely raise questions. After all, Victorians viewed incest as the gravest of sins. So, if incest was deemed evil, why did Maynard's and Mantle's mother-daughter roleplaying seem as erotic as their husband-wife roleplaying? Or is our view of their act presentist? Historian and queer scholar Julian Carter thinks so. Following Smith-Rosenberg's claim that multifarious intimac(ies) existed among Victorian women, Carter identifies one that emulated the nurturer-sensual mother-daughter relationship. If we deconstruct "Mother-Love," Carter argues, it materializes as a mentalité of *femininity* rather than sexual, which explains why it did not destabilize Victorian patriarchy.[65] Regardless, Maynard stands distinct in her dismantle of heteronormativity: "I pander to Amy's intense thirst for my love as her husband, as much as I enjoy listening to my 'daughter' talk about [heterosexual] romance." Her remark seemed redolent of Lock's, Mill's, and Bain's concept of sensations as a part of knowledge building; a sort of "consciousness beyond outside rule."[66] Accordingly, we might regard this curious Girton bond a highly valuable perspective on our present.

For Maynard, however, a far deeper concern than passion with Mantle in 1874 was class. She was crushed to discover that far from genteel, Mantle was illegitimate *and* "vulgar" as the ward of a very wealthy but "lowly" shopkeeper. Her shame was heightened by fellow Girtonians' scorn of her friendship with "a shoppy peer." Louisa Lumsden as a member of the gentry class "raged" at Maynard for her "stupidity." As an upper-middle-class woman, who called workers the lower orders, Maynard herself was "horrified; to *think* I have let her touch me and kiss me!" Yet she was caught between her class-based morality and romantic interest: "We cannot possibly be friends, but I [Maynard] cannot rebuke her clinging love."[67] Maynard's concern about class—though outweighed by desire and conversion—was evident in her remarks about Mantle. In January 1875, for example: "She's [Mantle] common and silly! She *thinks* that wearing white gloves makes her genteel! She even sleeps with them on!!"; and in May 1875: "Her want of tact jars me more than ever, so that I seldom want her with me, and feel as if I treat her very badly."[68]

In September 1875, however, when the new term began, Maynard suddenly voiced exuberance over Mantle: "My heart sings over Amy's radiant face in finding God!" Her language typified the Evangelical vocabulary of conversion that advised, for example, "[If] by the strong pressure of human love [you can] lead them [close friends] to Jesus, do it, do it!"[69] Yet at the same time, the green book invoked new discomfort over their physical passion. Maynard particularly fretted "over Amy's preference [to express] love for God" through daughter roleplaying.[70] Did Maynard now think this encounter abnormal? She did not elaborate, but she did react, her turn to Irving's Atonement theology a stark contradiction to her earlier religious language:

> For the past three years I have felt more conflict than ever before. I have *taken out all feeling*, all that makes Religion so lovable. I come to Thee with *bare intellect*. I am but a half-creature without Thee, useless, incomplete, and knowing in Thee is just that which satisfies my being. I mean to go at it, leaving absolutely everything else to Thee.[71]

One recalls Edward Irving's prediction for salvation: "We are under *complete* domination of three enemies, the flesh, the world, and Satan. Are we helpless? No, because God has left us Christ's Atonement, which is enough to employ us."[72] Like the girl who had prayed on prickly holly leaves, the older Maynard wished to prove her faith, this time, through the pain of celibacy. In October 1875, she wrote, "I told her [Mantle], 'You are of weak character. You *must* resist the human flame!'" Her addendum, "I feel our difference too strongly to admit any close tie," implies that class influenced her decision making. An angry, insulted, and frustrated Mantle "refused to turn [her] heart from [Maynard] to the Saviour. I love you too much to do *that*." Maynard pondered her dilemma: "I don't know how to behave for fear of grieving Amy, and I had vowed to take her on in both body and soul." Should she satisfy Mantle emotionally, or save her soul? Maynard chose the latter, leaving Mantle very distraught by a decision that diminished her well-being. In fact, Mantle failed her Little-Go examination.[73]

Our glimpse into Maynard's self-explorations intrigue, for they happened within the new autonomous college arena. Girtonians had opportunities to experiment with same-sex passion in the privacy of their rooms. Class seemed to drive Maynard's decision, but should we dismiss the possible influence of Bentham's, Locke's, and Bain's pleasure/pain principle? That is, the idea that "the pleasures and pains of experience led people, naturally and inevitably, to act in ways that increased their happiness."[74] Was Maynard's decision based upon her penchant for pain coupled with atonement thinking? We have discussed how such structures as the Victorian Church regulated sexual behavior for "sexually pure naïve" women. At the same time, historians of sexuality have shown how cultures of resistance opposed religious moral codes; for example, the movement towards birth control rights that began in the early 1900s.[75] Did college women form a culture of resistance against the dominant misogynist narrative? I would argue yes. Some scientists feared that college women's "male-aping corrupted their brains and may cause a complete biological sex reversal." Women did not biologically alter, women's colleges remained open and, eventually, *all* women entered the workforce.[76] Meanwhile, college women's private familial roleplaying at Girton may not have been enacted for gender reasons alone.

We see evidence of this sort of sensuality among college women in December 1875, when Maynard finally gave in to Amy's pleas:

> She [Mantle] drew me to her and I felt her heart beating so hard—when will anyone ever love me so much? She told me love was so strong—that it was as much as she could manage. That night she gave me all that I suppose one mortal *can* give away to another, and, holding her close,... I knew I *should* give her up to my Lord."[77]

Perhaps this Evangelical rhetoric was typical of a bond that ended when one woman completed her studies. They remained friends, and true to female norms, their friendship prepared Mantle for marriage. Maynard was particularly "happy to send [Amy] to the right [upper-class] man!" Nonetheless, her language is difficult to dismiss. Moreover, in 1919, she wrote: "I felt *discomfort* over Amy. I said, 'I cannot respond to the private side that gives you satisfaction.'" In Maynard's opinion, their passionate encounters were not simply a mistake. They were "wrong" probably on a sexual as well as a class level.[78] Still, there is no evidence of this conversation in Maynard's green book. We might conclude it a hindsight observation on her part. After all, by 1919, society could not fully ignore Ellis's theory of biological anomalies that now included female homosexuality, alongside sodomy. Ellis had interviewed women who admitted to same-sex sexual acts.[79] In 1875, however, when passion among women was tolerated, Maynard adopted symbolic language such as electric sparks or familial roleplaying to express her sexual feelings. We can only speculate on her actions and observations, but her dissonant voices tell us how complex a mindset can be.

The crucial task of understanding how past people thought returns us to history. We may only partially know a mindset, yet it reaffirms the importance of history-writing. Close attention to sources with the apt use of method produces valid accounts of the past. Facts can also change. Scholars largely agree that late Victorians maintained religiosity despite their crisis of faith, but Girton's college split uncovered an ambivalence about faith to be further explored. Nonetheless, Maynard (alongside extreme Evangelicals) still preached "Biblical Truth" based upon the Atonement, and conversion was core to her mission as God's prophet. She initiated a "Five Meeting" that instructed Bible study members to pray at 5:00 p.m. each Sunday. By 1876, this act of gathering was known as Maynard's Girton Prayer Meeting (G.P.M.). In 1905, the G.P.M. was amalgamated with the renowned Students' Christian Movement that retained an interest in missionary concerns.[80] Even so, Maynard's chide of careless agnosticism in 1902 relayed despair about her fate as Evangelical prophet amid the rapid growth of secularism.

We might question Maynard's "ardent conversion" of Mantle, whether or not Maynard thought she controlled her. Nor can we dismiss her angst over Mantle, given historians largely accede that passion among women was not stigmatized until the mid-1920s: when Ellis's, Freud's, and other's theories took firmer hold; and when single professional women chose to spend lives apart from men.[81] If Maynard did consider her acts with Mantle deviant in 1875, it seems possible that college women (and others) who transgressed female norms questioned same-sex feelings, and far earlier than historians think. At age eighty-four, a year before she died in 1935, Maynard read over her green book and autobiography and voiced perplexity at her past sexual naivety: "I look back on my life with a sort of compassion. I was in the full tide of youth."[82] The older, more sexually aware Maynard seemed irritated by a late-Victorian culture that kept women ignorant of sex and their bodies. Nonetheless, while she may have recognized her desires as a lesbian—the term was coined in 1921—the way that the younger Maynard contemplated passion and faith at Girton is a lesson to us. We might be astonished at how belief shaped her sense of divine privilege that in turn, influenced her worldview; her code of conduct; and her expression of love. As a pioneer student of the Mental and Moral Tripos, she wished she could "unite [her] confidence and passion" with her faith that denounced human will; but as she would repeatedly tell herself, "Yet, here lies the danger!"[83]

Notes

1. *Budget* Newsletter, 1902.
2. *A*, III, 11, "Girton, 1872," 355, written in 1919; and *GB*, 14 December 1871, 180.
3. For Lawrence see *GB*, 28 March 1871, 13, and for Girton *GB*, 20 June 1872, 85.
4. As mentioned, a few intellectuals knew of the new scientific discourses on sexuality in the mid-1920s, but mainstream society did not fully inculcate psychological theories of sex until the 1940s.
5. Quote taken from Firth, *Constance Louisa Maynard*, 110.
6. *GB*, 20 June 1873, 85. Girton, originally Hitchin, opened when Cambridge lecturers agreed to teach women. For more on Girton see, Rita Williams-Tullberg, *Women at Cambridge: A Men's University-Though of a Mixed Type* (London: Victor Gallancz, 1975),72.
7. *A*, III, 11, "Hitchin, 1872," 374, written in December 1915.
8. *D*, 28 October 1872, 88.
9. *D*, 18 January 1873, 78; and 26 June 1873, 111. See also Firth, *Constance Louisa Maynard*, 114.
10. *A*, III, 11, "My Years at Girton 1872," 355, written in October 1915.
11. See Constance Louisa Maynard, *Between College Terms* (London: James Nisbet, 1910).
12. See *D*, 13 October 1874, 67; 2 May 1875, 78; and 20 February 1874, 54. For more on these thinkers see, for example, Smith, *Between Mind and Nature*, 36–38.
13. Firth, *Constance Louisa Maynard*, 117–119.
14. Compare *A*, III, 11, "1872," 392, written in November 1915, with *GB*, 26 October 1872, 111.
15. *D*, 26 June 1872, 111, 116. For more on these thinkers, see Heyck, *Intellectual Life*, 190–195.
16. *GB*, 15 May 1873, 74. For more on Maynard's relationship with Louisa Lumsden, see Phipps, *Maynard's Passions*, 80–107. For the larger religious climate see Garnett, "Religious and Intellectual Life," in *The Nineteenth Century*, ed., Colin Matthew, 216–220.

17. *A*, III, 11, "My Years at Girton 1872," 353–355, written in October 1915.
18. See Richard Swindburne, *The Existence of God* (Oxford: Clarendon Press, 1979), 44.
19. *GB*, 12 November 1872, 242; 10 February 1873, 199; and *A*, III, 11, "My Years at Girton 1872," 360–361, written in October 1915.
20. *GB*, 16 September 1873, 144.
21. *GB*, 20 June 1874, 100. *D*, 18 June 1873, 88.
22. *A*, III, 14, "My Years at Girton," 488–515, written in December 1915. In 1873, after student increase, Hitchin relocated to a new building in Girton Village and was renamed Girton. For more, see M.E.T. *An Interior of Girton College* (London: London Association of Schoolmistresses 1876).
23. Quote taken from Firth, *Constance Louisa Maynard*, 57.
24. For more on this debate see Bebbington, *Evangelicalism*, 75–105.
25. See *GB*, 19 December 1873, 250; and 25 October 1875, 85. For more on free thought and feminism, see, Laura Schwartz, "The Bible and the Cause: Freethinking Feminists vs. Christianity, England 1870–1900," *Women: A Cultural Review*, 3 (2010), 266–271.
26. See *GB*, 23 December 1873, 260; 5 November 1874, 265; and 17 March 1875, 10.
27. *GB*, 16 January 1875, 69; and see also 17 March 1875, 10.
28. See *GB*, 23 December 1873, 260; 5 November 1874, 265; and April 1875, 54. See also King, *Reminiscences*, 30–31.
29. *GB*, 4 April 1875, 57.
30. See *GB*, 25 March 1874, 265; Firth, *Constance Louis Maynard*, 114; and for Victorians' religious crisis, see Heyck, *Intellectual Life*, 190–195.
31. See *GB*, 2 May 1875, 265, and 7 May 1875, 278.
32. *A*, III, 20, "Girton Years 1875," 605, written in June 1916.
33. *GB*, 22 June 1875, 182.
34. See *GB*, 6 June 1875, 176; and *A*, III, 20, "Girton Years 1875," 610, written in June 1916.
35. Compare *GB*, 22 June 1875, 182, with *A*, III, 20, "My Girton Years 1875," 610, written in June 1916. For the general decline in preaching on the Atonement see Bebbington, *Evangelicalism*, 144–147.
36. See *GB*, 6 June 1875, 176; 22 June 1875, 182; and *A*, III, 20, "My Girton Years 1875," 610, written in June 1916.
37. See *A*, III, 20, "Girton Years," 594, 616, written in June 1916; and Garnett, "Religious and Intellectual Life," in *The Nineteenth Century*, ed., Colin Matthew, 220.
38. For Victorian religiosity see Robin Gill, *The Myth of the Empty Church* (London: Society for Promoting Christian Knowledge, 1993).
39. For normal exception see Ginzburg, "Two or Three Things," 20.

40. See pioneer Girtonian Louisa Lumsden's, *Yellow Leaves: Memories of a Long Life* (Edinburgh: William Blackwood, 1933), 21–27.
41. Lumsden, *Yellow Leaves*, 7–15.
42. See *D*, 6 January 1900, 54; 4 May 1902, 99; and 9 October 1904, 231.
43. For the Annales and developments in historiography see George G. Iggers, *Historiography in the Twentieth Century: From Scientific Objectivity to the Postmodern Challenge* (London: Wesleyan University Press, 1997), 51–65.
44. Joan Wallach Scott, "Gender: A Useful Category of historical Analysis," *American Historical Review* 91, 5 (1986), 1053–1075. For recent work on women's history see, for example, Lara Campbell, Tamara Myers, and Adele Perry eds., *Rethinking Canada: The Promise of Women's History 7th edition*, (Oxford: Oxford University Press, 2016).
45. Compare Martha Vicinus 's *Intimate Friends: Women Who Loved Women, 1778–1928* (Chicago: University of Chicago Press, 2004) with Leila Rupp's "Toward a Global History of Same-Sex Sexuality," *Journal of the History of Sexuality* 10, 2 (2001), 287–302. For more on the topic, see, for example, Lisa Moore, "'Something More Tender Still Than Friendship': Romantic Friendship in Early-Nineteenth-Century England," *Feminist Studies* 18 (1992), 499–521.
46. Michel Foucault, *History of Sexuality Vol 1: An Introduction*, trans. R. Hurley (New York: Pantheon Books, 1985), 45, 60–66. Scholars find useful his concept of deviant sex as products of both social regulation and organization.
47. Davis, *Return of Martin Guerre*. Davis was curious about why an early modern French community accepted the missing Guerre's imposter.
48. See, for example, *GB*, 28 October 1882, 11, for Maynard's view on God and human will.
49. *GB*, 20 June 1873, 85.
50. *A*, III, 26, "My last Term at Girton, 1875," 699, written in 1918. For a good English edition of Kant's work see P. Guyer and A. Wood eds., *The Cambridge Edition of the Works of Immanuel Kant* (Cambridge: Cambridge University Press, 1992).
51. Compare *A*, III, 11, "1872," 392, written in November 1915, with *GB*, 26 October 1872, 111.
52. John Stuart Mill, *Autobiography* (New York: Columbia Press, 1924 [Originally published in 1873]), 70–79, 85. for Kant see Heyck, *Intellectual Life*, 166–186).
53. John Stuart Mill, *A System of Logic: Ratiocinative and Inductive* (London: Longhams and Green, 1906 [first published in 1843]). Mill refuted his father's and others practice of syllogisms that were usually represented in a three-line form: All men are mortal. Socrates is a man. Therefore, Socrates is mortal. For Mill, the principles of the natural sciences better explained

the mind because they speculated on natural phenomena and based their theories upon observation and experimentation.
54. Alexander Bain, *The Senses and the Intellect* (London: John W. Parker and Son, 1855), 5; *GB*, 20 June 1874, 100; and *D*, 18 June 1873, 88.
55. For discussion on the history of mental science, see Smith, *Between Mind and Nature*, 17. See also, A. Collins, 'England', in *The Oxford Handbook of the History of Psychology: Global Perspectives*, ed., D. B. Baker (New York: Oxford University Press, 2012), 182–210; and also, G. C. Bunn, A. D. Lovie, and G. D. Richards, eds., *Psychology in Britain: Historical Essays and Personal Reflections* (Leicester: John Wiley and Sons Ltd., 2001).
56. See, for example, *GB*, 23 December 1873, 260.
57. See *A*, 12, "My Years at Girton," 428, written in January 1919; and Vicinus' *Independent Women*, 158–159.
58. See *GB*, March 1870, 138.
59. *GB*, 20 June 1873, 85.
60. See Beasley, *Gender & Sexuality*, 117–127; and Doan, *Disturbing Practices*.
61. For more on binaries see Jagose, *Queer Theory*, 98.
62. For Mantle see *GB*, 7 March 1874, 90; and for the philosopher-theologian Paley, see *D*, 28 May 1874, 78.
63. Angharad Eyre, "Love, Passion, Conversion: Constance Maynard and Evangelical Missionary Writing," *Women's History Review*, 25, 2, (2016), 41, 47. Eyre also examined the writing of such missionaries as Harriet Newell.
64. *GB*, 10 May 1874, 245.
65. See, Saunders, *About Women, Love and Marriage*, 162; and Carter, "On Mother-Love," 131.
66. *GB*, 28 May 1884, 260; and 13 June 1884, 288. For Locke, see Heyck, *Intellectual Life*, 190–195.
67. *GB*, 26 April 1874, 200; and 10 May 1874, 245.
68. See *GB*, 12 January 1875, 36; and 14 May 1875, 266.
69. See *GB*, January 36, 1875, 78; and 19 September 1875, 98. For more on Evangelical vocabulary see Eyre, "Love, Passion,"44.
70. *GB*, 23 September 1875, 91.
71. *GB*, 26 September 1875, 98.
72. *GB*, 6 October 1871, 88.
73. See *GB*, 17 October 1875, 128; and 23 October 1875, 130.
74. See Bain, *Senses and Intellect*, 5.
75. See for example, June Rose, *Marie Stopes and the Sexual Revolution* (Boston: Faber and Faber, 1993).
76. See Weeks, *Sexuality, and Discontents*, 81, and for discourses on sex reversal, see Lisa Carstens, "Unbecoming Women: Sex Reversal in the Scientific Discourses on Female Deviance in Britain, 1880–1920," *Journal of the History of Sexuality*, 20, 1, (2011), 62–84.
77. *GB*, 29 December 1875, 198.

78. Compare *GB*, September 1881 with *A*, III, 25, "My Last Term, 1875," 763, written in July 1919.
79. See Ellis, *Sexual Inversion*.
80. *A*, III, 15, "My Girton Years 1874," 501, written in March 1916. Maynard's G.P.M. merged with the S.C.M. under the direction of Robert Wilder.
81. For debate on this, compare Porter and Hall, *The Facts of Life*, with Kingsley Kent, *Making Peace*. The former claim that changes in ideas about sex did not happen until the 1940s, while the latter proposes they were in place by the mid-1920s.
82. *GB*, 8 February 1934, 255.
83. *A*, VII, 62, "Long Vacation 1899," 448, written in June 1926.

CHAPTER 4

Difficult Relations, 1882–1891

Abstract Much has been written on how the cause, or the British nineteenth-century movement towards women's higher learning, dramatically altered women's lives. However, virtually nothing exists on how emergent professional educators coped with their new occupations within a patriarchal society. Chapter 4 addresses this lack, showcasing microhistorical events in 1882, 1884, and 1891 that illustrate Maynard's difficult Mistress-ship at Westfield College under her chiefly male administrators. More surprising, however, is Maynard's toxic relationship with a female Westfield Council member called Frances (Fanny) Metcalfe. In fact, their ongoing bitter relations expose heretofore unknown rivalry among the first female professionals. Unfortunately, their hostilities led Westfield Council to harshly discipline and ostracize Maynard for fifteen years, which explains how Victorians attributed professional competitiveness to masculinity.

Keywords The Cause • Clues and Innuendos • Female Professionalism • Female–female power

In 1915, Maynard emphatically told readers:

> My [Maynard] life is worth writing because it shews the inception and traces 'the cause'; a great national movement known as the higher education of women. The cause has placed professions within our reach, and doubtless has not yet attained its full growth. I fully believe that one day we will win the battle towards equality!![1]

Certainly, her autobiography brilliantly captured her important role in "the cause" towards women's rights to higher learning, a national movement to which she dedicated her life. What captivates, however, is how her records expose its sinister yet relatively unknown outcome: the qualified educator's newfound dilemmas with administrators. Chapter 3 explored how the minutia—Maynard's particular conflicts with science, faith, and love at Girton—unveiled intriguing aspects of the larger culture. This chapter continues the theme of women within higher education, but with focus on Maynard's trailblazing during the new phenomenon of "female expertise." We examine Maynard's intense acrimony with Frances (Fanny) Metcalfe, a member of the formally instituted committee that oversaw Westfield. We know little about Metcalfe or the other Westfield Council members. However, clues and innuendos proffer extraordinary insight into these new male–female and female–female affiliations. We begin with Maynard's journey towards the foundation of Westfield before turning to three tiny events in 1882, 1884, and 1891 that relay through Metcalfe the Council's harsh treatment of Maynard. From these unique cases, we glean unique insights into an era of disharmony over "cause-minded" women's entrance into professionalism.

In her overall view of the cause, Maynard summed the national movement noteworthy; and as we know, women's history has showcased the importance of female experience through the cause. Some historians also follow Maynard's view that the movement "was not one of steady progress." Deirdre Raftery, for example, traces how debates on female higher learning over two centuries gained momentum during women's labour opportunities in the 1880s. As Maynard further explained, the socio-political cause "placed many new professions within [women's] reach."[2] But she stood distinct as a committed educationalist even in adolescence. After leaving Belstead in 1866, she avoided what Emily Davies called, "girls' laborious trifling and … dissipation at home," by devising a "Bill" (work-timetable) to study such "male" subjects as Greek and Latin. That Maynard kept the Bill for four years was remarkable, not only because she assumed her formal education had ended. She was unaware that new girls' high schools and colleges had been established across the country during the late 1840s and early 1850s. These new institutions, among them the progressive London colleges, Bedford, and Cheltenham, forged for girls an education in the Classics and sciences regardless of "girls' accomplishments" taught at Belstead and other girls' schools until the 1920s.[3] And we know what happened in 1872 when Maynard learned of Girton.

Although Maynard's life-long pledge to the cause sprouted at Girton, her path was not easy. She negotiated Girton term by term with "promises to come home after [Tripos]."[4] In general, social opposition to the cause meant that relatively few college women sought careers. Maynard's love, Amy Mantle, exampled the many who returned home to marry. For her part, Maynard felt desperate upon leaving Girton in December 1875. Oakfield remained dominated by her ascetic mother whose debilitating asthma chained Dora to caregiving until Louisa died in February 1878. In addition, Harry's poor business dealings that jeopardized the family business caused great upset. Henry was disappointed with his son, but Harry's brother George never forgave him. Thus, in October 1876, an anxious Maynard planned a successful escape route to Cheltenham College. Her ex-Girtonian friend Louisa Lumsden who taught there wrote "a letter that implored [Maynard's] 'help' with marking Classics until Christmas."[5] In November 1876, Maynard, Lumsden, and another ex-Girtonian, Frances Dove, were offered salaried teaching positions at the new innovative girls' school at St. Andrews, in Scotland, to begin in September 1877. Maynard's parents abhorred the idea and so, she again said, "I am only 'assisting' friends," to downplay her emergence into professional teaching. Maynard remained at St. Leonards until she resigned in June 1880.[6]

"Cultivation"

Maynard's claim that the "inception of Westfield formed in [her] mind at Girton" carried through her interim years at Cheltenham and St. Leonards. She supported both schools' intellectual goals but deeply fretted over the "lax" religious teaching.[7] When back home, she received a "Divine sign" (about Westfield) through the newly formed Christian Women's Education Union (CWEU) that aimed to promote female missionaries overseas.[8] She knew a London-based college was crucial. The founding of University College in London in 1828 had usurped Oxbridge's education monopoly with entry limited to genteel male Anglicans. It had also proved a milestone in middle-class men's higher education with equal potential for middle-class women. In 1878, University College gained a supplemental charter, making it the first British university allowed to award degrees to women (except for medicine). Maynard believed this an opportunity not to be missed.[9] She wrote and presented at the CWEU in 1881 what became her well-known *Cultivation of the Intellect* that proclaimed literature, science, and religion were a comprehensive part of women's knowledge:

> Already we lament the secularizing tendency of so many of the best (intellectually speaking) schools, and already Christian parents shrink from them ... The common belief that women do not need cultivation is erroneous ... Attention must be given to places of instruction for girls – in whose hands the future of the womanhood of England lies.[10]

During an era in disarray over religious doubt and women's higher learning, Maynard's vision of cultivation—a combination of "female" moral piety and "male" university education—was forward-looking. Original educational pioneers such as Emily Davies proclaimed that higher learning "would make women better wives and mothers."[11] Some historians claim this tactic hindered the cause. Maynard, however, used Scripture to advocate for women's right to scientific learning: "The Bible shews that God brought the *whole* of human nature together—man and woman—and so, education should not separate human nature either."[12] Her (queer) dismantling of Victorian gender not only envisioned women's economic independence "from the bondage of marriage." Women would greatly *contribute* to the world of professionalism. Perhaps even more ambitious was Maynard's admonition that the educated girl was "the future of womanhood."[13] University-trained women would lead society from disbelief towards salvation. The problems of female domesticity and the crisis of faith would thus be resolved.

Maynard's discussion of *Cultivation* at the CWEU conference, in 1882, inspired a pious wealthy genteel spinster named Ann Dudin Brown to initiate in London a women's college that was Christian based. She immediately approached Maynard and said: "I have £10,000 for your college."[14] She then arranged a meeting with prominent London clergymen and Evangelical educators from which a "Westfield" Council was formed that consisted of Dudin Brown; the retired Colonel Martin Petrie; Dr. Thomas Boultbee, who was the Principal of St. Johns training ministry in Highbury; Canon James Fleming, who presided over St. Michael's parish in Chester Square; Dr. William Barlow, the Principal of a CMS institution in Clapham;

and Fanny Metcalfe, the co-proprietor of the well-regarded girls boarding school in Highbury. Maynard was voted in as Honorary Secretary.[15]

These Council members of whom little is written played a significant role in Maynard's strife at Westfield. Nonetheless, we learn more about their management of Westfield and indeed, Victorian culture, through the precious hand-written *Minutes of Westfield Council*. Maynard's diaries and autobiography, in turn, disclosed nuanced debates about a movement that threatened the late Victorians' concept of femininity and indeed, life as they knew it. For example, the green book of February 1882 bragged about Maynard's ability to persuade the Westfield Council against a domestic-missionary college: "We *must* reach Christians, but London's granting of degrees to women will *distinguish* your college.'"[16] The devout Council hesitated, however, not only because they typically knew nothing about running the new women's college, but they greatly feared what we might call scientific sexism.

Alongside scientists' claim that higher learning caused women's "biological sex reversal" was the well-known psychiatrist Henry Maudsley, who blamed the cause for "the rise in female hysteria [madness]." Meanwhile, the respected social reformer Lord Shaftsbury who attended the meeting declared: "The saddest part of my work is with fallen refined ladies." Some middle-class women "fell into prostitution" and so, he feared the cause would create more "evil."[17] His allegations were rooted in centuries-old ideas of women's weak physiology, but Maynard had dismissed them since Girton, and was determined. She first gained her father's support for the venture, and on 8 May 1882 triumphantly declared: "My unrelenting letters of plea to the Council worked." She was to be "First Mistress" of a college that was to be both religiously and academically based.[18]

"A Moral Domestic ... Corporate ... Hearth"

Before assuming what became thirty-two years of Mistress-ship (1882–1913), the thirty-two-year-old Maynard had to secure a building, students, and staff if the college was to be launched in October 1882. The Council's stipulation that she find a "country house" was not unusual. Emily Davies's Girton, for example, was leased from a country gentleman. Maynard was pleased to discover two three-storey terraced houses at Maresfield Terrace in rural Hampstead, a train ride from London. Her college would be a "moral domestic hearth [that emulated] male corporate life." The *Minutes* relayed the management of Dudin Brown's funds: "£630 for furniture, £210 wages for cook, housemaid, etc., and £500 for food for a year." Student room furniture estimated at £25 was typically late Victorian: "Writing table, 3 Black rush chairs, Little tea-table, Book-shelf, Chain-spring Bed, Hair-mattress, Japanese wash-stand, Glass bath, Toilet can, Rubbish pail, and Candles."[19] These room necessities of course relayed a time before the amenities of piped water, sewage, electricity, sanitized mattresses, and garbage collection. Maynard also endured nasty teething problems such as smoky chimneys and leaky windows. Nor had she any experience with what she called "inefficient domestics and multitudes of confusing bills that passed through [her] hands."[20]

Nonetheless, Maynard had a very clear vision for Westfield students. She first gained the Council's approval of the hybrid masculine–feminine rules adopted from Girton: "I [Maynard] said, 'I will tell students that we are corporate. They must use surnames and refrain from kissing in public. But I emphasized that permission was needed to travel alone, and that all male visitors were considered guests of the Mistress.'" The pious Council also supported her distinctive view of moral piety. This seemed surprising, for the Trust Deed approved by Dudin Brown advocated "Protestantism in harmony with the Doctrines of the Church of England." Certainly, there was an emphasis on the Bible as the most important part of religion. However, in contrast to Maynard's Biblicism, "the Doctrines" based on incarnational theology stipulated that Christ's Crucifixion saved Christians from Adam's sin. Maynard fully supported the idea of Westfield as the new academic institution, but for her, "the great task l[ay] in teaching and enforcing the Doctrine of the Atonement."[21]

The Council apparently agreed to Maynard's wish to ban worldliness. Westfield would not allow dancing, plays, singing, or parties, even though these typical activities were adopted at other new women's colleges in London and Oxbridge. Other upper-middle-class feminine ideals were, however, buttressed:

> [T]he open fireplace in each student's room; the maid with the bowl of water every morning; breakfast and lunch served in hot dishes on the service table; formal dress for dinner; prayers at night; the strawberry teas; the marmalade making; and the 'walking out' with a companion til' 1905, when we could walk alone.[22]

The Council was also reassured of Westfield's collective spirit. Like male college principals, Maynard sat at "the 'High' for dinner and the lecturer sat at a smaller table. It was unwritten law that no-one went twice consecutively to the same table. The same rule applied at night when students joined one another for tea, cakes, and jam."[23] Westfield's façade that beckoned daughters of pious genteel parents while exclusive, ultimately strove for societal acceptance. This goal was crucial since Westfield's degree program distinguished it from Oxbridge and the other London Colleges, Bedford, and Cheltenham.[24]

Westfield's trailblazing certainly created challenges that Maynard effectively surmounted. Her first term taught her that some parents viewed college as a means to rid difficult daughters. She tactfully handled one student's emotional breakdown alongside a wheelchair-bound student's needs, which slowed down the entire college. Meanwhile, prevailing attitudes led other parents to deem one term sufficient education for their daughter and so, finding recruits was a preoccupation and worry for both Maynard and the Council. For her part, Maynard was tireless in promoting Westfield. Alongside numerous letters to acquaintances and friends, her speeches at various girls' boarding schools and high schools across England helped Westfield to survive. Pioneering students who enrolled for the October, Lent, and May terms of 1882 and 1883 brought the total for the year to eleven. This sort of pattern was repeated year by year until the late 1880s, when society better accepted women's higher learning. A degree program (like that for boys) was expected to take three years to complete, and was Westfield's academic standard for many years.[25]

Another barrier to women's entrance into higher learning, and particularly the degree, was the inconsistency in girls' education that ranged from girls' accomplishments to private tuition. The latter equivalenced boys' high school curricula in preparing girls for Matriculation, which was a prerequisite examination for the University of London degree. Unfortunately, those trained in girls' accomplishments would inevitably fail Matriculation, given their lack in math, science, and language. The Council valiantly took the matter in hand by installing "Westfield's Entrance Examination." The examination required only a general knowledge of Scripture, history, geography, English grammar, and arithmetic. Maynard and her staff would then "work up" subjects for Matriculation, for example, the principles and practice of Euclid for mathematics. Students also studied Latin, Greek, French and German, English and English history, modern geography, natural philosophy, and chemistry. Success at the Matriculation level would distinguish between "General" students and those sitting the BA degree.[26] Westfield's program was piecemeal in Maynard's and the Council's search for suitable lectures, but the teaching arrangements were well suited to a college in process of building up academic work (Fig. 4.1).

However, while proud to be known as First Mistress of Westfield, Maynard was also quite nervous. She "felt keenly [her] insurmountable burden, for neither society nor Westfield Council would allow [her] to make mistakes." She also "feared being called home, but when [her] father visited Westfield that shred of doubt was cleared."[27] Yet, strangely enough,

Fig. 4.1 External view of the back garden at Maresfield Terrace with the Westfield College group, 1889. Courtesy of Queen Mary University of London Archives: Westfield College. Reference WFD/25/3/4. This image of Westfield's "annual garden party" examples how middle-class college women negotiated femininity with the masculine corporate. As Constance Maynard as Mistress pours tea, her resident staff members, Anne Richardson, and Mabel Beloe, seem prominent in the BA academic dress as graduates of the University of London. Maynard was denied the gown and cap because she completed her studies at Oxbridge.

apprehension did not dominate the green book. Throughout late 1882 and 1883, a frustrated Mistress raged over the Council's "ignorant opinions and decisions" that seemed shaped by the gender biases of a mostly male Council. She repeatedly argued the benefits of hiring Oxbridge or London-trained female resident lecturers, but they only agreed to one. Thus, while three external male lecturers each cost £130, Kate Kristram's salary of £70 as resident science lecturer included extra teaching and nightly supervision.[28] When the Council finally agreed to hire resident Classics lecturer Frances Gray in October 1883, Maynard's *Report of Mistress* proclaimed: "The cost per head for the BA has been lowered by £13!" Westfield had saved £86 in teaching, which was a lot of money at the time.[29]

This noted, Maynard was highly frustrated by the salary and work-based inequities between outside lecturers and her "exhausted" resident lecturers. And she felt similarly overburdened. She fully expected the Council's "agreement to a housekeeper, who only requested board. [She] had 'kept well in with them' and so, they would surely recognize [her] overwork as Mistress, Household Manager, and Honorary Secretary." The Council not only denied her request but scolded the disappointed Maynard about household expenses: "I [Maynard] kept silent and my heart sighed. I did not like to remind them [Council] that my father had contributed £1,000 towards the college."[30] The *Minutes*, diary, and autobiography conveyed "more wrangling" in 1883 over student enrollment, lectures, and household expenses. Maynard recalled leaving Council meetings in bitter tears over their criticism. What about the *Minutes*? Did they suggest the Council's disregard of the new female professional who struggled with leadership? It remains unclear. However, in Maynard's view, the Council not only demeaned her, but held Westfield back. She understood "that science [instigation of the BSc] was a priority at Westfield, and yet [the Council] only agreed after 'much hesitation.' These were very difficult years," Maynard concluded. "I was repressed by my Council in so many ways."[31]

Clues and Innuendoes: The Metcalfe Event, 1882

It is difficult to discern facts about Maynard's interactions with Westfield Council because most data about it is in Maynard's records. Moreover, this researcher's bias was evident before writing this chapter. My hypothesis was that Maynard's relations with her chiefly male Council would exemplify late-Victorian gender hierarchies. It did, but Maynard did not dwell upon male members as much as I expected. Nor is anything written about them and so, such angry snipes as: "Familiarity breeds *contempt* from those [Council] that feel so knowledgeable," did not necessarily infer men.[32] It thus seemed prudent to research and reassess female Council members. There were two: Ann Dudin Brown and Fanny Metcalfe. Little is written about benefactor Dudin Brown in the *Minutes* or Maynard's archive beyond her "grumbles over expenses."[33] The green book did however mention Fanny Metcalfe. She had supported Maynard's *Cultivation* in 1881 and had tirelessly helped Maynard to secure a suitable building for Westfield in 1882.[34] The elderly Metcalfe, it seemed, had befriended Maynard.

Metcalfe's support also included advice. Before assuming her Mistress-ship in 1882, Maynard mentioned without explanation: "Miss M [Metcalfe] has pressed me to offer myself without pay."[35] Metcalfe's guidance seemed unhelpful, even derogatory, given that the cause promoted women's professional independence. Yet, astonishingly, Metcalfe's sentiments echoed those in the *Minutes*. The differing salaries for outside male lecturers and resident female lecturers were listed, followed by, "Mistress guaranteed, as well as capitation."[36] That Maynard was initially unpaid was confirmed in her autobiography: "I worked for no salary for one year. I requested £50 during the second year, and £100 for the third year. My salary remained at that rate for several years."[37] Why had she agreed to work without pay? Her diaries were silent, and it was not until 1927 that she even offered an opinion: "They [the Council] *thought* that we [Maynard, Tristam, and Gray] got paid *enough* for the work we did ... I had asked for £50 because my dress allowance from home did not even cover expenses."[38] Notably, Maynard's initial request for a £50 "salary" was two-thirds of Gray's and Tristram's £75 per annum. Since she had fretted over her colleagues' workload and low salaries, nonchalance about her own seemed both puzzling and contradictory.

How might we analyze Maynard's salary dilemma? We may deem Metcalfe's and the Council's attitudes typical to the era. Elite women's work was generally assumed philanthropic. Still, it behooves us to interrogate a situation promulgated by Metcalfe that surely impacted relations between Maynard and the Council. The case particularly intrigues since nothing exists on unpaid educational pioneers and so, we have only hunches. But is this valid history? According to the pioneer microhistorian Carlo Ginzburg, conjecture was/is a powerful method if evidence is sparse. His coin of "the evidential paradigm" in the 1980s was loosely adapted from that of the pragmatist, Charles Sanders Peirce (1839–1914), whose theory of abduction was well regarded as a systemic method for sorting fragmented evidence into a workable paradigm. As the scholar Francis Reilly explains, Peirce's theory was a "process of framing and testing explanations of phenomena. Science progresses by ... imaginative leaps of abduction coupled with carefully controlled evaluation in the verification phase."[39]

In Ginzburg's view, Peirce's inferential method helps to facilitate historians' analyses of an obtuse event that at best is probably true. Inductive arguments are not as verifiable as deductive arguments, but they do require skills. Ginzburg likens the concept to a hunter's curiosity about a track that induces them to determine who/what made the tracks. Clues matter not so much because they are small parts of a bigger picture, but because they allow us to see something of the bigger picture which we would otherwise miss. The microhistorian then seeks more evidence about an unfathomable event by examining a range of analogous sources. "Fact" gathering, from this perspective, leads to a hypothesis about what possibly happened. The microhistorian might proffer only plausible conclusions, but they can be extraordinary glimpses into an otherwise opaque event.[40] It seems logical, then, to garner more evidence to endorse tenable verdicts on Maynard's stipend puzzle that give us insight into the larger culture. We might then add to this body of knowledge.

Let us begin to gather facts by examining the experiences of other first-generation late-Victorian female professionals. Historiography on this topic is very limited, but one recent study has highlighted why the few qualified late-Victorian female doctors disagreed over professionalism. As some adamantly declared that women worked only for "superior [religious] purposes," others challenged "unpaid gentrification by demanding decent pay."[41] Meanwhile, a study on newly qualified female astronomers exposed attitudes towards female scientists. The Royal Greenwich Observatory only hired women to replace computer boys—on the same menial salary of £4 per month that was difficult to live on.[42]

Westfield's first graduates further highlighted women's plight. The Church Missionary Society had begun to hire qualified female missionaries, yet still called them "voluntary helpmates" to their male counterparts.[43] The genteel Council held similar views about Maynard's role. Why? If we re-consider the note in the *Minutes*: "Mistress guaranteed, as well as capitation," we might speculate that both Council and Maynard agreed to the latter's salary if the scheme went.[44] Maynard's father's view of dress allowance and "entitlement to call [her] home" implied his favor of the philanthropic arrangement. Or did father, Council, and Maynard view her Mistress-ship as that for religious (superior) purposes?

Our evidence indicates that it was a combination of all of the above and thus, we may concede that Maynard's world was very different from our own. Nevertheless, she fumed over an "ignorant" Council who criticized her. Certainly, she and the Council coordinated college rules, resident lecturers, and the BSc. Other late Victorians also supported professional women; for example, the progressive Cavendish laboratory in Cambridge encouraged male–female collaboration in scientific research.[45] Even so, the Cavendish male community (like the Church Missionary Society) ultimately deemed female counterparts "helpers," and their thoughts echoed the Council's attitude towards Maynard.

In general, late-Victorian professionalism and work remained masculinized and even influenced working-class ideals. Factory men, for instance, were paid more for the so-called skilled task of working machinery than women were for "unskilled" intricate lace-making. Moreover, working women (like middle-class women) faced sanctions if they engaged in "unfeminine" behavior even when disrespected by superiors. For example, a group of linen factory girls "dared" to remove their tops and dance provocatively around their director to embarrass him for demeaning them.[46] Our clue has uncovered historical roots of a past that has only been partially resolved by society. Today, women of all classes and race face harassment and disrespect at the workplace. Nor do women always receive the same pay as men. Historical narrative explains the past and in so doing foretells what might be done in the future. From the minutiae, this microhistorian drew insights relevant to contemporary concerns about gender discrimination and bias.

THE METCALFE EVENT, 1884

Maynard's relations with Metcalfe vastly deteriorated after Maynard began her unpaid position as Mistress in October 1882: "Murmurs from Miss Metcalfe," Maynard lamented: "She accuses me of staunch Evangelicalism!"[47] Perhaps Metcalfe opposed Maynard's faith because her boarding school, Highbury, encouraged girls to sing and dance. Or did her concerns go deeper? The green book did not explain. Nor was anything written in the autobiography. Meanwhile, the diary held little hope. Entries about events were usually unfathomable unless Maynard discussed them elsewhere. But what we might call serendipity, prevailed, for a close investigation of the diary uncovered an increase in Metcalfe's "murmurs" about various college issues during and after 1883. She appeared to have become the Council's messenger with unannounced visits to Westfield to "generally scold" Maynard. What Maynard came to call their "dispute ins" in 1884 ranged from student admission to household matters. After one nasty altercation about "expenses" Maynard exclaimed, "I have *seldom* been so angry!" Another expostulated: "She [Metcalfe] is so antagonistic that I can barely control my-self under her 'lordly' air."[48]

Maynard was perhaps a poor manager in contrast to Metcalfe, who had gained skills in administration as a Girton Council member and co-proprietor of Highbury. Nonetheless, Maynard knew that her fury with Metcalfe aside, she must display affability to maintain her superiors' and indeed, late-Victorian support. After all, Davies had repeatedly and wisely advised Girtonians to "convince society that [they] were *entirely* feminine in manner."[49] Yet, unfortunately, Maynard's fight for power and respect—rather like that at Girton with free thought—led to disaster at a Council meeting in December 1884. Maynard lost all control when the "lordly Miss M began to reprimand [her] for poor book-keeping." What Maynard said to Metcalfe or what happened after her verbal outrage was not recorded in any records. Even so, the green book relayed that Maynard "felt so *uneasy* about [her] *disgrace* that [she] quickly apologized to the Council" to try and appease them. However, she was not only severely sanctioned but also ostracized. Dudin Brown's "fit of pique" about the event, which forced Maynard to relinquish her seat on the Council, triggered a series of harsh penalties enforced by the Council.[50]

They first clipped the "dissentious" Maynard's wings by instituting subcommittees for household management, college promotion, student admission, and faculty recruitment. In a corporate setting, these subcommittees could have greatly benefitted Maynard had she been male. But the opposite happened. The *Minutes* conveyed that the Council then appointed a secretary in Maynard's place and told her: "You are no longer entitled to be present at Council meetings." Maynard thought them mistaken, for nothing was written down. Nonetheless, her name came off the Trust Deed and her only communication with the Council was through a written end-of-term *Report of Mistress*.[51] As a result, she had no say in important decisions made by Council members throughout the term. In essence, she became a figurehead who did not even receive advanced copies of Council agendas. Needless to say, pressing matters like contagious outbreaks or resident lecturer anxieties were either dismissed or not resolved. In fact, Maynard found herself bereft of support from a Council who now blamed her for most problems. Throughout the mid- to late 1880s, her anger interchanged with shame over her mistake with Metcalfe. She "felt beholden to the Council's decision," and the ways in which she confronted her mistake—anger, shame, and finally, bitter resignation—relayed her cultural context. She was all too aware that symptoms of female hysteria included stereotypical notions of "the angry female deviant."[52] We cannot be surprised that Maynard considered resigning to flee her unpleasant situation.

This noted, it would be remiss not to further investigate Maynard's account of her tensions with Metcalfe and Westfield Council. After all, there is little in the *Minutes* beyond mention of the instigation of subcommittees and Maynard's end-of-term report. We should therefore be mindful of Maynard's bias as well as this historian's account of her "plight." We might wonder if Metcalfe and the Council were rightfully wary of Maynard's volatility. Or possibly, as Maynard's biographer Catherine Firth claimed, Maynard "at times unwittingly exaggerated their unkindness." Even so, as a former Westfield student who knew of the volatile situation, Firth told readers that Metcalfe's "lack of sympathy and carping criticism caused Maynard much unhappiness."[53] Firth's comments seem potent because her biography did not otherwise dwell on Maynard's Mistress-ship, Westfield, Metcalfe, or the Council; indeed, one reviewer of Firth's biography wanted "to read more facts about the college."[54]

Janet Sondheimer's *Castle Adamant* (1983), which carefully traced Westfield's history as a new women's institution, adopted a feminist-based empathy for Maynard's "resentment at the Council's treatment of her." Sondheimer did not mention Maynard's issues with Metcalfe but in her opinion, "the Council came to recognize the awkwardness of their arrangement."[55] Yet Maynard did not attend Council meetings until 1899. Moreover, the Council only granted her full membership in 1913 out of respect for her successor. In short, their modification of Westfield's initial goals as a Christian-based academic college went unimpeded as Maynard was rendered mute. Whether misguided, or deliberate, the Council's "arrangements" born from the disastrous Council meeting demeaned and controlled Maynard, who "bore the affront in silence for the sake of the college."[56] Her difficult relations are a vital contribution to the historiography on early female professionalism since we know little of this past. Some readers may be shocked by the outcome of acrimony between a first-generation professional educator and her female superior. Far from finding facts about united, cause-minded women, through Maynard, we have uncovered elements of female–female discord that subordinated one educational pioneer for fifteen years.

THE METCALFE EVENT, 1891

Unfortunately, Maynard's hostilities with Metcalfe remained, and from them sprang another startling clue from a diary entry written on 6 April 1891. At the time, Maynard was overseeing Westfield's relocation to house the now forty-four students. She not only disliked moving from the cozy terraced houses to the more corporate arena of Kidderpore mansion. She felt both humiliated and angry that Westfield Council had not consulted her about their choice. The new Westfield "was *not*, by the *widest* stretch, the confiding college [she] had devised."[57] She was further upset when a quarrel with the resident lecturer, friend, (and possible lover) Frances Gray led the latter to recant on assisting with the move. But this paled in comparison to Metcalfe's surprise visit during the disorganized move and haughty criticism of it. We have no details of their encounter except that Metcalfe, nonplussed about Maynard's plight, angrily called her a "weak leader, who lack[ed] duty to [her] faith."[58]

We know that Metcalfe had criticized Maynard's management of Westfield. But what about her attack on Maynard's faith? Metcalfe's remark made little sense, for to that point she had deemed Maynard's evangelicalism *staunch*. So, what lay behind Metcalfe's new concerns? The diary did not explain; the autobiography was silent; and sadly, the green book had ceased (it tapered off in 1887 and did not resume until 1901). Gone thus are potentially rich elucidations about Maynard's life experiences in the 1890s. No one can explain the missing green book but, whatever the case, it reminds us that "gaps" in an archive can exist and that history is partial and fragmented. We have mentioned the historian's responsibility to determine what the creators of sources intended. In this instance, we have little sense of Maynard's feelings at the time, or later, as we did with Girton's split. Yet Metcalfe's remark *seemed* a summation of her overall disfavor with Maynard over the years (Figs. 4.2 and 4.3).

We may solve this event if we return to Ginzburg's evidential paradigm and consider Metcalfe's remark within linguistics. Let us begin by asking, did Metcalfe's accusation concern religion or academics? Or was it a combination of both? But *Maynard* wrote this sentence. So, what might it

Fig. 4.2 External view of Kidderpore, the white neo-Classical stucco mansion to the far right, which became the "second" Westfield in 1891. Courtesy of Queen Mary University of London Archives/Westfield College/WFD. Reference WFD/25/3/1.

have meant to *her*? It proves difficult, for as the anthropologist Clifford Geertz explains, we "*strain* to read words over the shoulders of those to whom they properly belong." His analogy bespoke the linguistic turn, which was a key movement in the 1970s that inspired academics to draw upon disciplines like anthropology to interpret a culture's social habits or knowledge systems.-[59] For their part, historians claimed that language was the key to explaining the past, but they also understood that its meaning could never be truly known.[60] We found useful Darnton's insights into "elusive language" in our analyses of Maynard's remarks about Hetty Lawrence. In this instance, we might conjecture that Maynard's diary entry about the move invoked the gist of Metcalfe's accusations, or at least what *Maynard* understood from them.

Fig. 4.3 Westfield College (at Kidderpore), 1894, showing the group of forty eight students and three lecturers. Maynard, who particularly disliked Westfield's "secularist" ionic columns, is seated in the middle of the first row wearing her white lace cap. Courtesy of Queen Mary University of London Archives/Westfield College/WFD. Reference WFD/25/3/1.

We know that Maynard had since girlhood consistently used the term "duty" to explain her commitment to faith. Both she and the Council had firmly agreed that Westfield would interrelate faith and higher learning. We might thus wonder if Metcalfe thought Westfield's fundamental aim had been compromised. Our best plan forward then, is to *backtrack* in search of a tenable explanation for Metcalfe's acrimony. Strangely enough, working backwards is a fascinating and logical aspect of tracking clues. For one, a vague comment makes little sense unless we know what preceded it; and two, we better comprehend the pressure of the past on Maynard.[61] In terms of "duty," let us pause on Westfield as a newly opened college in October 1882 when Maynard voiced delight over a local sermon that advised "Christians to walk alone through the bad streets with the Lord Jesus.'" The sermon inspired Westfield's motto based upon Edward

Irving's *Parable of the Sower* that warned Christians: "The good seed is wasted if hearts are already occupied with worldliness."[62] Maynard had however assured the Council that as promised, she would link Irving's theology with higher learning; in this case, Immanuel Kant's concept of reason as the means to morality. But in 1891, she guiltily told readers that she had emphasized faith-based morality (resisting worldly sentiment) over rational thought.[63] Perhaps the Council knew of this and so, Metcalfe's accusation concerned Maynard's change of direction in her religious-philosophical teaching.

Certainly, Maynard's preference for genteel clergyman's daughters at Westfield was problematic for the Council, which possibly augmented their ostracization of her for over a decade. At a "terrible meeting in 1884 [she wrote], the Council rebuked my narrow vision."[64] It was at this meeting that Maynard lost control when Metcalfe accused her of poor bookkeeping. In 1886, her attempt "to admit only Ladies to Westfield" was denied. In fact, it seems possible that the Metcalfe event of 1884 had hardened the Council's disregard of Maynard's wishes. They immediately instituted a clause that would "determine whether the Candidate [was] 'desirable' to college." The clause, which granted Council the right to admit what Maynard called, "terrible city [middle class] girls," aimed to raise enrollment and convey Westfield's new corporate image. Maynard, meanwhile, clung to Westfield's original aim: send university-trained genteel pious women to fight the "extreme [and worsening] crisis of belief."[65]

The Council's ensuing debate over "whether Westfield was equivalent to that of Bedford and Cheltenham," cemented the divergence between Mistress and Council. Bedford and Cheltenham were now officially affiliated with the University of London, and the Council wanted Westfield to become "'a School' of a university that advocated a Liberal education based upon scientific observations."[66] We might speculate that the Council's shift from Westfield's initial aims caused Metcalfe to denigrate Maynard's leadership in 1891. However, our conjecture would have flaws. Assuredly, Maynard's discrimination of "terrible city girls" echoed her calling Amy Mantle the "vulgar" daughter of a wealthy shopkeeper. Still, she did not abandon Mantle, and classism did not prevent Maynard from supporting all Westfield students and their academic goals. Westfield's graduates had not only pursued missionary work overseas. Of the two dozen who had graduated, more than half had gained the BA; five in Classics; three in French; two in Physiology; and two in Geology. Four had secured lectureships while the remainder taught at new girls' high schools.[67] This suggested a Mistress who had consistently supported her students' secularist goals, whatever their class.

Perhaps because the Council had control of Westfield's public goals, Metcalfe as "Council messenger" was tasked to spy on Westfield's interior. The Council could then modify internal traditions as they saw fit. Let us again backtrack to Westfield's early years. According to the *Minutes*, the Council never interfered with this aspect of Westfield. But they strongly reacted to one incident. When Classics lecturer Frances Gray asked to leave residence in October 1885, Maynard was immediately summoned to the one (five-minute) Council meeting that she attended until 1895. We learn little from the *Minutes* except that Maynard's plea for another resident lecturer was quickly denied. The Council stipulated that Gray "was to be 'Visitor lecturer,' and full-salaried." After the meeting, Maynard wrote: "I could almost read their nasty thoughts, but I'm sure they are wrong."[68]

Maynard never explained her comment, but the green book did mention that Gray had not only accused Maynard of "overworking [her]," she also voiced discomfort over Maynard's "*personal* absorption" in her. Maynard's "final word" to Gray in December 1885 seemed a faith-based pretext: "When anyone is called to the kind of work, I [Maynard] do, it is very lonely, but one can satisfy that loneliness with God's permission."[69] In any event, the green book lost momentum after Maynard's conversation with Gray and ceased on 30 August 1887 until 1 January 1901. Whether deliberately destroyed, or lost, this huge gap in Maynard's archive highlights the challenge of clues. However, we might wonder if Gray discussed Maynard's behavior with the Council, who then confronted Maynard about it at the short meeting in 1885. The event possibly left Metcalfe suspicious of Westfield's interior with Maynard at the helm, which triggered her outburst in 1891 when Maynard seemed incapable of garnering either staff or students to help with Westfield's move (Fig. 4.4).

Even so, we cannot verify Metcalfe's or the Council's thoughts. Nor had they acted in 1885 and after. Our best plan forward, therefore, would be to gather supplementary evidence about Metcalfe's opinion of Westfield's interior. One recent study about Westfield claims that Maynard's authority waned in the early 1890s as students began to challenge her college rules, such as "walking out alone."[70] We could surmise that this fired Metcalfe's criticism of Maynard's weak leadership in 1891. Yet Maynard feared her loss of control as early as 1884. Gray's disfavor of Westfield's ban of dancing and plays, for example, was told through Maynard's sad lament over their "least provocation." Gray who had left

Fig. 4.4 Early Westfield College Group, 1885, at Maresfield Terrace, at full capacity with eighteen students, three Resident staff members, and Maynard, aged thirty-six, who is center of the second row. Kate Tristram is to Maynard's left, and staff member Frances Gray is to her right with a book on her lap. Courtesy of Queen Mary University of London Archives/Westfield College/WFD. Reference WFD/25/3/1.

residence in 1885 moved back in October 1890 to perhaps renew her relations with Maynard. However, their bond was destroyed in January 1891, when the Council asked Gray to relocate early to Kidderpore with a few students. Perhaps the Council wished to give Gray an opportunity at leadership or felt Maynard as Mistress should oversee Westfield's bigger overhaul to a new building. In any event, after Gray moved, she introduced the dances and plays she had argued for in 1884, and when Maynard found out, she angrily accused Gray of "destroying [her] confiding college."[71] Gray retaliated by going home for Easter and informing the Council of her wish to leave residence (again). It was after this event that Metcalfe attacked Maynard during said move to Kidderpore.

A Plausible Verdict

While our interrogation into the Metcalfe events have not produced concrete answers, we might speculate that they were combinations of the above evidence presented. Underlying difficult relations was a struggling female professional who faced barriers with Metcalfe and a Council new to managing a women's college. The Council's goal to forge Westfield's success as a scientific institution was clearly at odds with Maynard's cling to its original religious-academic aim. In terms of leadership, Maynard seemed to avoid enforcing rules if staff or students challenged them. Her emotional needs were also questionable. The Council via Metcalfe possibly assessed Westfield's interior and Gray's flight from residence in 1885, and again in 1891, yet they took no action against Maynard. In this, sources can help us to understand past thoughts in ways that their authors never intended. That the *Minutes* did not mention such terms as "sexism," "equity in pay," or "sexual misconduct" imply such concepts were unfamiliar to late Victorians, let alone female professionals. Of course, without full disclosure in either Maynard's archives or *Minutes,* the genesis of Metcalfe's issues with Maynard remain unclear.

Nonetheless, we can identify positive outcomes of Maynard's early Mistress-ship and the Metcalfe events. Her invitation to Council meetings once a term in 1895 gave her some leverage. While she now knew to silently endure the Council's displeasure over such issues as student failures, she could verbally demand higher salaries and reduced teaching loads from eighteen to sixteen hours per week. Other changes were also evident. The student body now stood at fifty with four resident lecturers in place. Of the fifty students enrolled, over half aimed to take the BA or BSc.[72]

Westfield seemed to symbolize society's move towards secularism and equality between the genders. However, the success of Maynard's Girton Prayer Meeting was apparent in its metamorphosis into the well-respected Student's Christian Movement; a huge organization that relayed the Victorians' vested interest in maintaining faith. Moreover, sadly, the deep-seated sexist classism within Westfield's community remained. When the Council in 1889 raised resident lecturer salaries to £150—an increase of £80 since 1882—the *Minutes* included Maynard's philanthropic-like offer which, oddly enough, reflected Metcalfe's advice in 1882: "I [Maynard] truly hope the Council won't take amiss, that, knowing present straits for funds, I should be glad if they would subtract £50 from my salary." The Council agreed, and "would revisit the matter in another year."[73] One hopes that Maynard was earning at least £150 per annum by then.

"Difficult Relations" has illuminated the striking omission in historiography on the power struggles distinct to first-generation professional women, in this case, the tensions between Maynard and female members of a restrictive Westfield Council. This suggests that like Girton college women, professional women were ambitious. Readers have discovered that clues and even silence shine a light on an obscure past. Maynard's interactions with Metcalfe and the Council suggest society's wrestle to maintain tradition and religiosity in face of women's higher education. For example, elite female philanthropy impeded women's autonomy that, in turn, appeared to influence professional women's support of each other. First-generation female doctors disagreed over aim, while Metcalfe and Maynard seemed caught between traditional femininity and personal ambition. We also learn that the cause intersected with larger conflicts about religious doubt, secularism, social mobility, and women's higher learning. Ultimately, Maynard's vision for autonomous women through cultivation—deemed outmoded by Metcalfe and the Council—was both realized and normalized after 1891 with increases in qualified, single, professional Westfield women. Readers might ponder the workings of Westfield (and perhaps other new female institutions), but they gain insights into how Maynard and others gained economic independence and thus freedom for prescribed femininity.

NOTES

1. *A*, 1, 1, "1849–1860," 1, written in 1915.
2. *A*, I, 1, "1849–1860," 3, written in 1915; Deirdre Raftery, "The Opening of Higher Education to Women in Nineteenth Century England: 'Unexpected Revolution' or Inevitable Change?" *Higher Education Quarterly* 56, 4 (2002), 331. See also June Purvis, *A History of Women's Education in England* (Bristol: Open University Press, 1991), 73.
3. For Maynard's Bill, see *D*, 4 March 1871, 6; 6 March 1871, 8; and 10 March 1871, 10. For the development of girls' education, see Alice Zimmern's classic, *The Renaissance of Girls' Education in England: A Record of Fifty Years' Progress* (London: A. D. Innes, 1898).
4. *A*, III, 11, "My Years at Girton 1872," 355, written in October 1915.
5. *D*, 25 July 1876, 89.
6. For Maynard's work at Cheltenham and St. Leonards with ex-Girtonians Louisa Lumsden and Frances Dove, see Phipps, *Maynard's Passions*, 80–107; and Vicinus, *Independent Women*.
7. *A*, III, 11, "Girton, 1872," 374, written in December 1915.
8. For the C.W.E.U. see Caroline Cavendish, *Aims for Higher Education* (London: Simmons and Botten, 1881), 7–13.
9. In contrast to Oxbridge, the University of London was an examining body only with no imposed residential requirement on candidates (Heyck, *Intellectual Life*, 166–186).
10. Constance Maynard, *The Cultivation of the Intellect* (London: Westfield College, 1888), 7, 18.
11. Davies, *Thoughts*, 102.
12. Maynard, *We Women*, 130. Quote modified from Gal. III: 28, 657. For more on educational pioneer's tactics see Ellen Jordan, "Making Good Wives and Mothers? The Transformation of Middle-Class Girls' Education," *History of Education Quarterly* 31, 4 (1991), 444–445.
13. Maynard, *Cultivation* 7.
14. *GB*, 12 January 1882, 28.
15. *GB*, 6 February 1882, 38. Solicitor Sidney Gedge who replaced Dr. Boultbee in 1884 was a member of Executive Committee of the CMS (Sondheimer, *Castle Adamant*, 12–22).
16. *GB*, 12 February 1882, 41.
17. See Henry Maudsley, "Sex in Mind and in Education," *Fortnightly Review* 15 (1874), 466–468; and for other scientific ideas, Carstens, "Unbecoming Women," 62–63.
18. *GB*, 16 April 1882, 82.

19. *Minutes of Council*, 1882, 4, Special Collections, Courtesy of Queen Mary University of London Archives/Westfield/WFD. Hereafter cited as *Minutes*, plus date and page numbers).
20. *A*, VII, 44, "My Life's Work, 1882," 4, written in May 1925.
21. *A*, VII, 44, "My Life's Work, 1882," 7, 9–10 written in May 1925; *Minutes*, 1882, 6; and Sondheimer, *Castle Adamant*, 39.
22. Firth, *Constance Louisa Maynard*, 251–252.
23. Letter to Janet Sondheimer, 25 March 1976, from F. Lyle in reply to letter 16 March 1976, Ms. 317, Special Collections, Courtesy of Queen Mary University of London Archives/Westfield College/WFD.
24. As noted earlier, "Girtonians" were angry that their exams, which were the same as men's, did not count as degrees *because* they were women. Cambridge did not grant women degrees until 1948. The London based Bedford, Cheltenham, and Royal Holloway colleges would follow Westfield in preparing students for university degrees.
25. *A*, VII, 44, "MY Life's Work," 46–50, written in June 1925. See also Sarah Burstall, *Retrospect and Prospect: Sixty Years of Women's Education*, (London: Longmans Green, 1933).
26. *Minutes*, 10 May 1899, 294; and Sondheimer, *Castle Adamant*, 30–34. The first Westfield students enrolled before sitting the Entrance Examination.
27. *GB*, 30 September 1882, 41–49.
28. See *GB*, 22 October 1882, 56, and 12 November 1883, 80. For Maynard's tactics to secure the Cheltenham trained Kate Tristram, compare *Minutes*, 2 July 1882, with *GB*, 30 June 1882, 41.
29. "Report of Mistress," in *Minutes*, October Term, 1883, 88–91. The Newnham trained Gray taught elementary Classics while Tristram taught elementary science.
30. *A*, VII, 39, "Autumn Term 1883," 40–42, written in April 1926.
31. See *A*, VII, 43, "May Term 1883," 60–63, 68, written in December 1926; *D*, 3 June 1883, 120; and *Minutes*, 3 June 1883, 156.
32. See, for example, *D*, 22 June 1882, 78; and *GB*, 28 March 1883, 76.
33. *GB*, 22 October 1882, 61; and 8 December 1884, 302–304.
34. See, *GB*, 6 February 1881, 38; 12 May 1882, 66; and 18 May 1882, 70.
35. *GB*, 26 May 1882, 90, 167.
36. *Minutes*, 1882, 4.
37. *A*, VII, 46, "Introduction to 31 Years as Mistress," 2, 59, written in May 1926.
38. *A*, VII, 43, "Autumn Term" 1883, 69, written in June 1927.
39. Francis E. Reilly, *Charles Peirce's Theory of Scientific Method* (Fordham: Fordham University Press, 1970), 60.
40. Carlo Ginzburg, *Clues, Myths, and the Historical Method*, trans. John and Anne C. Tedeschi (Baltimore: Johns Hopkins Press 1989), 105. See also

Wilson, *History in Crisis? Recent Directions in Historiography* 3rd edition *(New Jersey: Pearson Education*, 2014), 75–76.
41. Vanessa Heggie, "Women Doctors and Lady Nurses: Class, Education, and the Professional Victorian Woman," *Bulletin of the History of Medicine* 89, 2 (2015), 274, 268–270.
42. Marilyn Bailey Ogilvie, "Obligatory Amateurs: British Women Astronomers at the Dawn of Professional Astronomy," *The British Journal for the History of Science* 33, 1 (2000), 67, 73. Victorian "computer" individuals trained in plate-glass photography to chart stars and other celestial objects.
43. See *A*, 1883, "My Life Work," 59, 62, written in May 1926; and Jenny Daggers, "Transforming Christian Womanhood: Female Sexuality and Church Missionary Society Encounters in the Niger Mission, Onitsha," *Victorian Review* 37, 2 (2011), 89–106. The C.M.S. had since the 1870s received complaints from male missionaries regarding lack of pay for their qualified wives.
44. *Minutes*, 1882, 4.
45. See Paula Gould, "Women and the Culture of University Physics in Late Nineteenth-Century Cambridge," *The British Journal for the History of Science* 30, 2 (1997), 120–137.
46. See Laura Frader "Doing Capitalism's Work," in *Becoming Visible*, eds., Bridenthal, Stuard, and Weisner, 295–326, 313, for more on Victorian capitalism, gender, and class.
47. See *GB*, 1 October 1882, 167.
48. *D*, 22 October 1882, 78; 19 September 1883, 24; 7 March 1884, 19; and 12 September 1884, 29.
49. Lumsden, *Yellow Leaves:* 1–15; 21–7.
50. *GB*, 31 December 1884, 302–304.
51. *Minutes*, I August 1884," 49; and VII, 55, "May Term, 1884," 50, written in December 1927.
52. *A*, VII, 55, "May Term, 1884," 88–89, written in December 1927; Sondheimer, *Castle Adamant*, 38–39; and for female anger see Maudsley, "Sex in Mind," 466–468.
53. Firth, *Constance Louisa Maynard*, 199, 273.
54. Eleanor MacDougall, Review of *Constance Louisa Maynard, Mistress of Westfield College*, by Catherine B. Firth, *Westfield College Magazine* (1949), 15. MacDougall was lecturer between 1902–1912.
55. Sondheimer, *Castle Adamant*, 40.
56. *GB*, 26 March 1884, 55; 11 October 1885, 97, and Sondheimer, *Castle Adamant*, 41.
57. *A*, VII, 53, "May Term 1891," 287, written in October 1927.
58. *D*, 23 April 1891, 89.
59. Tosh ed., *Historians on History*, 315–324.

60. The origins of "the cultural turn," which is quite complex, included Marxist social history (EP Thompson); postmodernist thinking; the post structuralism of thinkers like Roland Barthes and Michel Foucault; the insights of cultural historians like Robert Darnton, and anthropologists like Clifford Geertz, who assumed the idea of "otherness" (Wilson, *History In Crisis?* 117–118).
61. See Ginzburg, *Clues, Myths, and Historical Method*, 105. For more on clues, see Peter Burke, "History of Events and the Revival of Narrative," in *New Perspectives on Historical Writing, 2nd Edition*, ed., Peter Burke (Pennsylvania Polity Press, 2001), 295.
62. *GB*, 8 October 1882, 21.
63. Compare *GB*, 21 December 1883, 56 with 16 October 1891, 88 and 1 November 1899, 99. For more on Kant and others, see S.J. McGrath and Joseph Carew eds., *Rethinking German Idealism* (New York: Palgrave Macmillan, 2016).
64. *GB*, 31 December 1884, 302–304.
65. See *D*, 6 March 1886, 122, for Maynard's perspective. For the Council's, see *Minutes*, 4 May 1886, 74.
66. *Minutes*, 6 November 1886, 120
67. Sondheimer, *Castle Adamant*, 42.
68. See *Minutes*, October 1885, 45. For Maynard's remarks about the Council, see *GB*, 12 December 1885, 199.
69. *GB*, 20 December 1885, 94. For more on Maynard's relationship with Gray see Phipps, *Maynard's Passions*, 126–151.
70. Lisa Robertson, "'We Must Advance, We Must Expand': Architectural and Social Challenges to the Domestic Model at the College for Ladies at Westfield," *Women's History Review* 25, 1, (2016), 114.
71. See *GB*, 20 December 1885, 94; *D*, 23 February 1890, 89; and *A*, VII, 53, "May Term 1891, 286, written in October 1927.
72. See *Report of Mistress* in *Minutes*, 8 July 1895, 26; and *A*, VII, 49, "October Term 1895," 177, written in May 1927.
73. See *Minutes*, 7 April 1886, 208; and 9 April 1889, 234.

CHAPTER 5

Colonial Affairs, 1897–1904

Abstract Chapter 5 explores two micro-historical incidents in 1898 and 1902 to convey how Maynard's patriotic prophetism shaped her intimacy and subjugation of Marion Wakefield, an Irish Westfield student half her age. Coincidentally, Maynard's idiosyncratic articulation of faith was rooted in South African Calvinism. Sadly, her sense of power as Mistress, English, and prophet damaged Wakefield's health and self-esteem. Regardless, Maynard fully believed that Wakefield's Irishness was in dire need of "civilization" and conversion. Historians analyze how an idea like Englishness created domination among people, both nationally and globally; however, few explore how pious patriotism shaped sex feelings among British women. Maynard's relationship with Wakefield may appall readers, yet it symbolized late-Victorian concern over global control in the fin de siècle.

Keywords Empire and Civilization • Irishness and Englishness • Queer theory • Calvinism • Female Prophetism

In an upbeat account of ambition and ideas, the pious Maynard exclaimed:

> Never be afraid of having an idea! I [Maynard] have only one idea and it begins with a W. If the idea is 'a girl' or a 'School,' that is big enough to embrace everything, because the being has a body, and a mind with an imagination, and affections, and a conscience, and an immortal soul; and that embraces just about all earth and all Heavan.[1]

Her choice of "W" to explain the importance of "an idea" would not seem enigmatic to former Westfield students reading her circulatory (budget) newsletter in 1903. They would assume that W meant Westfield's distinct cultivation or intellectual moral piety for creating professional women. They also knew that Maynard's "calling" to combat worldly disbelief had inspired her theology program at Westfield in 1901. They might not, however, have known that the "W girl" to whom the fifty-four-year-old Maynard assigned attributes like affections and conscience, was thirty-one-year-old Marion Wakefield; a former Westfield student who was now Maynard's Secretary, but was on leave after her second emotional breakdown as Maynard's five-year lover. Wakefield could not tolerate Maynard's ascetic renouncement of their passion. She ended their bond in 1904.

This chapter's "colonial affairs" introduces Westfield's particular imperialist culture under the older pious Maynard to illustrate how concern over empire influenced college women. We also examine how a profound "Englishness" shaped Maynard's attitude towards the young Irish Wakefield. When their intimacy deepened and bordered on the sexual, the devout Maynard advocated celibacy, prayer, and fasting; unusual actions that caused Wakefield's acute breakdowns. These tiny events that inspire exploration into Maynard's behavior not only uncover its astonishing origins in her father's South African Calvinism. We learn that the Maynard-Wakefield bond embodied larger concerns in England during the fin de siècle.

When we zoom in on Maynard's life in 1897, six years after the last Metcalfe event, she tells us, "The sky is clear!" Her family had survived her brother Harry's loss of family wealth, her father's sudden death in 1888, and the sale of Oakfield and land in the mid-1890s. Gone for the most part were Maynard's complex difficulties with Westfield Council. She had been allowed to attend end-of-term Council meetings since 1895. In 1899, she attended them all. Well-qualified second-generation university women now taught Classics and science at Westfield. And 1897 was another "successful Capping year" with nine graduations, including Westfield's first MA.[2] Westfield's genteel, conservative etiquette remained and would continue until Maynard retired in 1913. She was described as a kindly Mistress who liked "social customs and connected to students through games of 'Snatch' [Scrabble]." She still adopted strategies to gain support for the cause by reinforcing upper-middle-class femininity. For example, the performative tone of Westfield's early years was embodied in Westfield's rose gardens and the annual "At Home" that hosted up to 500 genteel guests with fine dainties, china, rented furniture, and orchestra.[3]

Alongside cultivation, Westfield boasted a curious "Character-building" that students attained through theological, scientific, and nationalist thinking. Maynard's idea of character certainly invoked the late-Victorian imperialist era, as exemplified by topics for Westfield's monthly debate. In 1897, Maynard's diary exclaimed: "Spoke about governing the colonies! Imperial Federation won by a *great* majority, of *course!*" The Imperial Federation League of 1884 had aimed to inaugurate one federal state over Britain's colonies to dismantle such self-governing colonies as the Cape of Good Hope (South Africa) and the Canadas (British North America). Notably, however, Westfield's debate happened three years after the League's collapse in 1894. Maynard wished to instill in students the "crisis of empire" and thought the debate highly successful: "Character had informed students' wise decision. England must rule degenerates [colonized native peoples]."[4]

Not all Westfield students shared Maynard's views. Irene Biss recalled her successful defense of "a Bill allowing 5 shillings weekly to poor people out of work. I'm [Biss] *glad* to say that the votes were in favour!" She was likely unaware of Maynard's thrill over the motion lost for socialism five years earlier. Maynard's low opinion of English workers had not changed either.[5] Nonetheless, her term "degenerates," echoed middle-class concerns about English society and empire. Certainly, the state sought to standardize education for all working men and eventually, women, to create a nation of cooperating citizens. Anglicizing the colonized and securing territory was a different matter. British leaders' vigorous defense of imperial interests was symbolized by the second South African War (1899–1902); a war won but one that resulted in attrition and humiliation.[6] Meanwhile, colonial governors anxiously prodded missionaries to "civilize" native tribes, such as the Pondo, and Maynard too, was keen to participate in the Pondo mission. After all, her father had lived and traded at the Cape, and her brother Harry had inaugurated the South African Steamship Company.[7]

Maynard's new travel diary characterized "'Pondoland' [Pondo tribe] as an inveterate idle [evil] people … doomed to die out before the incoming [English] force!"[8] At Girton, she had vehemently condemned "evil" science, including Darwinism. Yet science now bolstered her faith and empire-mindedness. Just as she envisioned the idle Pondo's crumble before the English, so imperialist Darwinists alleged that "England's push of the weak to the wall was a beneficent process."[9] The younger Maynard had inculcated her father's Malthusian-like beliefs formed at the Cape. The clergyman Thomas Malthus (we recall) had warned how overpopulation could outstrip food supply, thus to "artificially feed" the destitute "went against laws of nature" and divine grace. Colonists had utilized Malthus's classist ideals to predict that "lowly" primitives could not survive if they opposed (white) Christian civilization. Maynard's calling the Pondo idle, and doomed, however, seemed to merge Malthus with Darwin's later ideas. Indeed, as Darwin claimed, his "theory of evolution was the doctrine of Malthus;" but of course, Darwin challenged Biblical Creation while the pious Malthus had not.[10]

By the late 1870s, Darwin and other evolutionists such as Thomas Huxley and Herbert Spencer had firmly agreed that "primitives" were "less evolved" than the average Englishman. Primitives lacked the ability to think, and so, there were "inferior" and "superior" people. Even as Spencer warned his colleagues of the "biases that impede[d] scientific observation," he still observed that "the lighter skinned people [were] habitually the dominant ones."[11] However, not all scientists had maintained their fervor for evolution theories. In *Wonderful Century* (1898), Alfred Russel Wallace mulled over "the scramble for Africa. The result, so far, has been the vast sale of rum, gunpowder, and much bloodshed owing to the objection of the natives to the seizure of their lands and their cattle." He was less willing than Darwin, Huxley, and Spencer to biologize or naturalize capitalism, war, and imperialism. He found offensive the idea that "extinction" of the indigenous was inevitable due to white "progress."[12]

Meanwhile, Maynard's vision for Sunday Function (meeting) at Westfield highlighted her more unique interconnection of empire with science and faith. Students, for example, learned the crucial need of Westfield missionaries in white settler colonies, such as the Cape, to "rightfully" maintain the British empire. Her enthusiasm for global consolidation bespoke the aims of the former Imperial Federation. She also applauded organizations like the Student Voluntary Missionary Union, and the British Colleges Christian Union that promoted the goals of the Bible League to maintain the reverent study of the Holy Scriptures.[13] The Bible

League was of course a defense against the Liberalist, capitalist, and scientific age. As Wallace attacked theories of evolution, other groups like agnostics, unitarians, and free thought challenged Biblicism that promulgated white bias in British colonies. Regardless, the imperialist Maynard still maintained that the "*Truth* [Bible] shewed God's natural distinction [race]." She fully believed that no righteous superior English Christian like herself "could bow" beneath such a yoke.[14] Through faith, Maynard carved her own "Englishness" to ground her sense of self. She constructed who she was as an individual and with whom she should associate.

IRISHNESS AND SAME-SEX FEELING

If forty-eight-year old Maynard had "fierce 'Englishness,'" then "Irishness" was clearly an embarrassment in her choice of twenty-five year old Marion Wakefield. Certainly, Maynard's accounts of her intimacy with Wakefield will seem ghastly aspects of late-Victorian culture. Nonetheless, rather like the topics addressed in Westfield's debates, Maynard's views epitomized English concern. We have addressed the reliability of sources about small, obscure events. Wakefield, unfortunately, left no personal sources behind, and we have no identified images of her. Let us, therefore, establish facts about the Maynard–Wakefield bond from Maynard's archive though, as we recall, her green book from this time is missing. As Maynard "compress[ed] [her] green book account into two or three incidents in [her] autobiography" sadly, much of the detail is lost. In any event, we learn that she first met Wakefield in April 1897 at her organized Easter retreat in Berka, Holland:

> My [Maynard] first impression was not favourable. Marion was crude, abrupt, and easy going, and I found her difficult to be around ... However, in about a week ... the Irish openness confronted with English reserve, and she became more deferent towards those who were either older or wiser than herself.[15]

Maynard's condemnation of Wakefield's Irishness implied sovereignty over Wakefield, the unequal other; and Ireland did indeed have an anomalous position in the British empire. While an integral part of the British metropole, the country was subject to English militarism on its soil and an English majority in parliament structured its economy. Many English people considered the Irish almost as backward-looking as South Africans, deeming both unfit to self-govern.[16] Some openly denigrated the Irish, for example, Darwinians warned that revitalized Irish Romanizing

(Catholicism) would cause degeneration. Meanwhile, Parliament in 1886 and 1893 quashed Irish Home Rule in the claim that it would disintegrate the British empire.[17] For the anti-socialist, Unionist, and proudly English Maynard, the empire required the political inclusion of and yet subjection of the Irish. English militant labourers and socialists, of course, deferred to the upper classes.

After she had "tamed" and purportedly reconciled herself to Wakefield's Irishness, Maynard's autobiography characterized falling in love through a Hellenist-religious language that (like "electric sparks" with Hetty Lawrence) seemed unfamiliar for the time. She did so by transcribing one green book entry which, written in May 1897, presumably best conveyed her past feelings:

> What a glorious thing love was! The colours grew brilliant as I thought of it. All the while Christ stood beside me, offering me white, pure white ... I must choose white, and I will, I dread love ... She [Wakefield] had come to us so recklessly happy, and now, tears on her cheeks ... Here I am tearing her soul to pieces. Am I a Minotaur that I must eat a maiden's heart?[18]

Although Christ offered her white (purity), the imperialist Maynard as mythical half-man half-bull metaphorically devoured Wakefield's bodily and spiritual substance. The Hellenist gods gave the Minotaur freedom to rule land and sea and granted his every wish. Maynard, therefore, had permission to tear apart the maiden. Thus, far from submitting her will to God, Maynard's unfettered control relayed agency, which once again questions her alleged "hate" of Mental Philosophy at Girton that "burdened" her.[19] In fact, we may wonder if John Locke's intriguing idea of "consciousness beyond outside [social] rule" inspired her imagined Minotaur-evangelist (Figs. 5.1 and 5.2).[20]

"Queering" the Minotaur-evangelist helps us to better understand the multiplicity of Maynard's sexual self-consciousness. In this, Sharon Marcus's dismantling of Victorian heteronormativity in *Between Women* (2007) uncovered curious forms of female–female aggression. Her queer analysis of fashion magazines, for instance, revealed to her young women who gazed suggestively at each other's breasts, while demure young women seated next to stern female elders implied forms of erotic dominance.[21] From this, we may propose that Girton's faith-science split was as distinct a form of female–female domination as Maynard's imagined role as Minotaur-evangelist. In fact, according to the scholars Frederick Roden

Fig. 5.1 Constance Maynard aged forty-eight, 1897, seated at her desk in the Mistress's room. Courtesy of Queen Mary University of London Archives/ Westfield College/WFD. Reference WFD/1/1/2.

and Yopie Prins, a revived Classicism in the late 1890s inspired a handful of pious women to imagine same-sex feelings. Prins notes that the educational pioneer Jane Harrison's ponder of ancient Greek sex mores led her to declare: "I think this fleshy [same sex] desire must be felt and lived [rather than] intellectually analyzed!" In Roden's and others' view, these sorts of micro-investigative processes deconstructed heteronormativity and heralded the broader language of homosexuality in the fin de siècle.[22]

Fig. 5.2 Constance Maynard aged forty-nine, 1898, with Westfield group. Maynard is seated second row in center with long-term colleague Anne Richardson next to her on her right. Possibly, Marion Wakefield is seated next to Anne Richardson. The young woman resembles Maynard's description of her, was Richardson's niece, and did enroll at Westfield in 1898. Courtesy of Queen Mary University of London Archives/Westfield College/WFD. Reference WFD/25/3/1.

We do not know for certain who or what influenced Maynard and can only hypothesize. Yet at Girton and now, at Westfield, her multiple shifts in sexual self-consciousness produced by faith and intellectualism afforded her an unusual form of control over college women's emotions. For her part, Wakefield, who was "a forceful spiritual influence in Portadown in Northern Ireland" questioned belief under Maynard's stern asceticism. Moreover, she (like other college women before her) seemed victim to Maynard's sexual ploys: "I [Maynard] hated myself for having brought her [Wakefield] to this sorrow. But there was that thrill, the actual physical sensation of the sinking of my heart. I was *not* going to walk away ... God was near, and I felt a wave of extraordinary sweetness and peace."[23] Maynard's ongoing comments implied that she caused Wakefield pain, though she assured readers that her conduct was faith-based. Even so, her thoughts recall Alexander Bain's and John Locke's philosophical pain/

pleasure principle, and intriguing ideas of the individual's "consciousness without conscience, open to the winds of change."[24] However, we cannot fully determine their influence since Maynard did not separate sex from faith or science. Nor can we discern whether Wakefield was a willing participant, or even verify the validity of Maynard's account.

What we do know, however, is that Wakefield did not immediately attend Westfield, and that Maynard often visited the dilapidated Wakefield estate in what she snobbishly called, the "desolate bog-land of Portadown." When Wakefield did enroll at Westfield in May 1898, she "was there to reach out to." Maynard added, "I could not resist her tall slender frame, creamy skin, cloudless blue eyes, splendid blonde hair, and full red lips." Wakefield apparently "responded with a full heart on fire ... It was endless, 'Oh Mistress, I *love* you, I *love* you!'"[25] Inseparable during college terms, a trip to the Pyrenees in April 1899 invoked their private world of love: "Sometimes Marion bathed, a snow-white Naiad, while I kept watch. After she dressed, we would lie together on the warm turf." This mythical beautiful naked Naiad, it seemed, gave life to waters. That she might also drown an ardent lover implied that Wakefield also exercised sexual power.

Regardless, after a year of what seemed a passionate, intense bond, Maynard began to fear that their physicality was "far, *far* too much." After telling readers, "I should hide my head in shame," she transcribed another green book entry, written in May 1899: "*I* am supposed to take the steady side since it is *I* who has lighted M's fire. Oh! Let us try for Passion pure in snowy bloom through all the years of blood!" Maynard's resolve to their mistake was harsh if we compare it to her Girton love, Amy Mantle. Her advocation of celibacy and prayer with the added pressure of fasting severely impacted the infirm Wakefield, and her studies. She left in June 1899 to regroup from anxiety, and weight loss, angrily telling Maynard: "I hate suffering. I play at it for your sake. But I do not *want* to believe in self-denial or 'the death of the self' with its wills and desires. This is impossible!"[26] Wakefield thought suppression of passion was inherently wrong while Maynard seemed overwhelmed by their possibly sexual relations. Her autobiography continued, "I *could not* write about her for a year. When I did, I poured out my heart in over twenty pages."[27] Without Maynard's green book, we cannot know what she recorded in the late 1890s. But she wrote her autobiography in 1929, when the sexologist Havelock Ellis's term, "female homosexuality," challenged the culture of female friendship. Therefore, we may wonder if Maynard or another consequently destroyed a diary that described homosexual acts; Maynard often "fe[lt] inclined to burn it [green book]."[28]

Yet if this was the case, why transcribe green book passages in her autobiography that she hoped to publish in the late 1920s? Not only had a few late-Victorian women utilized ancient sex mores to explore "lesbian" desire before the term was known. A few others had boldly characterized sex acts through flora; the word "bloom" invoked the arousal of the clitoris.[29] If Maynard knew of this same-sex erotic language in the late 1890s, her try for passion pure in snowy bloom may have been an analogy for chastity. Did she insist upon celibacy ("snowy pure" clitoris) with Wakefield after "years of blood" (engorged clitoris)? Or was passion pure about devoutness, not sex? Surely it was the latter if Maynard wished to publish her autobiography. Even if a new female homosexual language *did* exist in the late 1890s, piety was still a part of female friendship.

Still, though, Maynard recalled her mistake through specific (we might say explicit) green book entries to perhaps avoid hindsight thoughts about her past sex feelings. Or do we read too much into her language? After all, some scholars propose that the concept, lesbian, was not widely understood in society until the 1940s, a decade after Maynard wrote her autobiography. We may consider what the historian Anna Clark calls the "twilight metaphor" as a conceptual tool to fill a gap to describe sexual relationships, desires, and practices that were neither celebrated nor utterly forbidden; behaviors that were not fully articulated by those who engaged in them. Maynard could not conceive her desires through a term (lesbian) that would initially profoundly stigmatize and shame female–female sexual acts. Nonetheless, stigmatization, or not, Maynard still felt that she "should hide [her] head in shame." As we learned from the linguistic turn, language constrains interpretation. We can never fully know its true meaning and can only produce partial accounts of the past.[30] Maynard's rhetoric raises provocative questions that we cannot fully answer.

What about Maynard's other writing at the time? Does it provide more evidence? Or answers? We noted that her travel diary adopted science to condemn the Pondo tribe. In contrast, her newsletter to OS implied late-Victorian ideas about faith and culture to reveal her incidental challenge of sex norms. She commended "missionaries' island of chasteness amid polluted seas [Pondo]" yet exclaimed: "I love the 'wild' place!" Quite possibly, she secretly admired "the [Pondo's] unabashed sexuality." Even so, excessive sexuality was in the end an attribute of another culture. Following Wakefield's emotional breakdown, the newsletter reminded OS about how pious chaste women *should* conduct themselves. The Pondo women's "coming out rituals" at the "marriageable age" were sexually deviant; their bodily movements became sensual and sly, "and in every way dreadful."[31]

Yet, as discriminatory as Maynard seemed about Pondo women, she seemed to anguish over her own conduct with Wakefield. In January 1900, seven months after Wakefield fled Westfield, Maynard took a six-month leave from Westfield to recuperate from fatigue (and perhaps guilt). She immediately "tracked down the ailing" Wakefield in Switzerland and their "tryst" promised love and hope. She then declared that a trip to Egypt "had revived [her] faith" and her calling as God's prophet. She returned to Westfield in May 1900 with a "deep longing" to initiate a theology program at Westfield with Wakefield by her side.[32]

Thinking About Thoughts: The Roots of Prophetism

We may infer from our queer approach to Maynard's various documents that a "fluid" Englishness pervaded her notions of faith, sexuality, and femininity to shape her feelings about Wakefield. Nowadays, her actions may infuriate us if we designate her a "racist" bully who emotionally abused her young student lover. Even so, we must be mindful of how ideas about nation and empire strongly impacted her. This does not exonerate her behavior, but nor should we assign blame. So, what can we write? Some theorists claim that scholars have no right to interpret personal experience, but historians believe themselves trained to do so. Yet, as we noted when we interrogated the Maynard–Mantle bond, historians shy from analyzing female–female domination through pain.[33]

Studies of women and empire also tend to discount patriotic dominant women. This is not to dismiss pioneers of the field who in the 1980s highlighted how histories about empire largely featured men. More recently, scholars have effectively utilized "gender" as a tool to trace how women either resisted or acquiesced to masculinized imperialism. Ann Laura Stoler and others, meanwhile, have identified how binaries like metropole/colony reify and categorize societies.[34] Certainly, we can agree that both colonized *and* European nineteenth-century female bodies were regulated, surveyed, and disciplined. Yet, this theoretical focus often characterizes European women as pious prudes, who engaged in sex movements like social purity or eugenics that regulated sexuality.[35]

Maynard supported social purity, but her self-reflections, that were multifarious and fluid, invoked sexual agency. When she contrasted her "pure Englishness" with "dreadful Pondoland" and "crude Irishness," she not only explored and expressed sex feeling through faith. Through the layers of empire—English, Irish, and colony—she imagined sexual power through the "wild place (colony)," the imperialist-Hellenistic male-like Minotaur trope, and her "calling."[36] Still, we know little about why nation and empire connected to Maynard's life-long sense as a prophet. God called her in adolescence, and this profound feeling shaped her experiences at Girton, and beyond. Since we have not yet explored the genesis of Maynard's powerful vision, let us place it under the microscope to see if we feel differently about Maynard's behavior when we return to her bond with Wakefield.

We can start by asking, can we even explore the roots of a patriotic prophetess who embraced suffering for worldly feelings? As we know, exploring the intangible can produce only speculation. But according to philosopher and historian R.G. Collingwood, we might alter our opinion about past individuals if we explore their visceral experiences. In his view, facts of history are useful only to uncover past mindsets. Writing before the linguistic turn, cultural history, and queer theory, his influential writings published posthumously in *The Idea of History* (1946) claimed the uniqueness of history in recovering the human condition. Collingwood has since been criticized for insisting that historians can recreate past thinking without bias or due consideration to the historical context. Nonetheless, he has inspired historians to dig deeper by asking new questions.

We have shown how new information about Maynard's Tripos helped us to better analyze her mindset and experiences. When turning to her faith, we might assume it emanated from her mother's repressive preaching on Irving's theology. The elderly Maynard certainly blamed her mother for "untold mental damage." But is this the entire story of her faith? What about her sense as God's prophet? Her mother always condemned such thinking as "egotistic, foolish, and sentimental." Who, then, shaped Maynard's unwavering calling as "God's Chosen"?[37] And why did it connect to the empire?

The beginning of an answer to this may be in Maynard's biographer Catherine Firth's remark: "It seems unlikely that ... even Louisa [Maynard] weakened Henry [Maynard's] belief [in] total human depravity." Firth did not further explain, but Henry undeniably was Calvinist-thinking in belief "that all [were] born 'depraved' from Adam's Fall."[38] The green book of 1867 and 1869 also revealed Henry's belief in those chosen by God, for three prominent entries invoked his impassions for what he called, "live prophets."[39] Did Henry's South African experiences therefore include encounters with a colonial-like Calvinism? Does this explain the patriotic Maynard's intense imperialism? We cannot fully know since Henry left no records behind. So, how might we further explore this? We might consider Collingwood's belief that facts can recover an individual's thought processes, especially if we do so in conjunction with Carlo Ginzburg's view that speculation, based upon clues, is part of historians' skills.[40] Their ideas, which correlate with a queer approach to identity formation, help us to better dismantle, explore, and speculate upon Maynard's sense of being chosen by God.

Maynard's documented conversations with her father Henry, such as about living prophets or theologians who felt chosen by God, provide circumstantial rather than verifiable evidence of her feelings. Nonetheless, Maynard's thoughts are windows into her own experiences as well as those of Henry. We recall that at age fourteen (1863) she ruminated from the prophet Isaiah to claim: "A real prophet is needed now ... to fight worldliness itself."[41] Four years later, in 1867, she wrote of her father's devotion to Calvinist theologian Thomas Erskine of Linlathen who, according to Henry, believed that God chose individuals for certain tasks. Not much else is written on Erskine.[42] However, just as God called Maynard at fourteen and again at twenty-two (at Girton) to found what became Westfield in 1882, so Calvinists believed that "God's elect willingly followed God's bidding." Many Calvinists believed Isaiah to be a prophecy of Jesus's Crucifixion to save humankind. Maynard, in turn, thought she was "a live Isaiah," called to save the world from sinfulness.[43] From the evidence that we have on the roots of her power-based "masculinized" prophetism, it seems logical to hypothesize that Henry influenced her calling. To proceed with this investigation, we will gather more evidence about Henry's colonial past while focusing on religion.

Henry Maynard's family was among those pioneering English imperial merchants who began trading overseas commodities in the 1700s and thereafter. In 1819, as Britain gloried in the global control of politics and economics, Henry and his brother Charles sailed to South Africa to work as agents of the firm of their powerful uncle, Henry Nourse. The brothers set up business in Grahamstown, the Cape to successfully trade in building materials, liquor, sugar, tobacco, and wool for eighteen years, until Henry returned to England to marry Louisa in 1837.[44] Henry as noted did not record life at Grahamstown or his early trading business; and according to both Maynard and Firth, he never discussed it after marriage either.[45] However, while this gap is serious, we may utilize Ginzburg's evidential paradigm to proffer inductive inferences about an obtuse past. If we amass evidence on Grahamstown written by others of the same class and time, we may hypothesize that their experiences were similar to Henry's.

The records of the English traveler, Thomas Baines, are especially instructive alongside the diaries of pioneer geologist Mary Bowker, whose upper-middle-class family possibly sailed with the Maynards from England to the Cape in 1819 and settled in Grahamstown. We learn from Baines that the white settlement of 4,000 people at the time had a transplanted English environment, with thatched houses and cobble-stone streets, a large market area for trade, and regularly laid-out roads converging on the Church.[46] Mary Bowker as an English-born female lacked a formal education, though she excelled as a natural historian at the Cape.[47] Whether Henry knew the Bowkers or Grahamstown's science society is unknown, but he introduced his children to the sciences of geology, botany, and astronomy. While most elite fathers expected daughters to marry and remain home, Henry was extraordinary in support of two daughters' careers: Dora in nursing and Constance in education. In other words, Bowker's and Baines's sources provide evidence to speculate about Grahamstown's positive influence on Henry's views of women's professional capabilities.

The history of Cape Calvinism itself generates further clues about Henry Maynard. The original white Cape settlers in the 1600s were mostly Dutch Calvinists, known collectively as Boers. Their belief as "chosen" not only legitimized the slaves they brought with them but justified appropriating land and enslaving thousands of pagan African tribespeople. Calvinists believed that the very mind, will, emotions, and flesh of the pagan were so corrupted by sin, and therefore, so "evil," that they could not be saved. And, notably, Boer Calvinism matured in a mixed-race vacuum apart from European Enlightenment philosophies of reason, individualism, and skepticism. Change happened in the early 1800s when the British arrived. Historians note that the Boers' demeanor as chosen regressed to one of suffering after the loss of the Cape to the English in 1814. However, when the English abolished slavery in 1833, the remaining Boers in Grahamstown were enraged because they conceived slavery as economically viable in the hierarchy of Creation. The Calvinist doctrine of election [had] come to serve as a crucial legitimation for racial inequality… The Bible proved that the idea of freed *pagan* slaves as "equal" to Christians [white Europeans] was contrary to [God's] natural distinction [of race]. No decent Christian could bow beneath such a yoke.[48]

We recall here Maynard's sentiment mentioned above: "*Truth* [Bible] shews God's natural distinction [race]," which suggests ties to Boer Calvinism. Nonetheless, Maynard and her family (like most mid- to late-Victorians) opposed slavery; and for their part, English colonists condemned the Boers' economic- and faith-based justification of slavery. Meanwhile, the Boers criticized English legal double standards for penalizing non-English labourers.[49] It seems that both European groups ultimately dominated non-whites in the region and so, ongoing clusters of tension over faith and race may have engulfed Henry.

The idea of "empire" was clearly complex and in this, the historians Antionette Burton and Tony Ballantyne explain "webs of empire" as bound to trade, knowledge, religion, migration, military power, and political intervention that intersected with categories like class, gender, and race. Webs of empire sanctioned certain groups' sovereignty over others; English webs we recall, connected to science like Smith's *Wealth of Nations*, which conceived progress through the link of economics, social organization, and (middle class white) "Character," while Malthus's prediction on the "plight" of population created other forms of hierarchies around race, class, and religion.[50] As Burton and Ballantyne note, empire webs were fragile, and could modify. However, if we dismantle conqueror/conqueror, we recognize that scientific, social, and religious ideas would have cast "conquerors" like Henry "superior" to the Boers who were, in turn, "above" the colonized "evil" primitive "savages." At the same time, the Boers rationalized English control of the Cape as God's test for some divine task. Whether oppressors as slave-owners, or oppressed after defeat by the English, they held God's sovereignty as God's elect. Faith was the medium through which the Boers negotiated the various imperialist systems of domination. In fact, Cape Boer Calvinism impacted numerous white settlers' lives over time and even continues to this day.[51]

If we perceive empire meta-binaries as fluid, and acknowledge the influence of Cape Boer Calvinism, it seems possible that a Boer-English shared Calvinism existed. Henry did not support slavery as the Boers did, but his scientific concept of African tribespeople as savages, rather than human, perhaps had affinity with the Boers' interpretation of unconditional election. Sadly, we cannot substantiate these claims, for no one has written about a Boer-English shared Calvinism in the 1820s and 1830s. Nonetheless, historians have recently challenged overarching secularist accounts of the English empire. They claim that empire-minded Oxbridge intellectuals during and after the 1820s promulgated unconditional election: God's secret plan was revealed through the "special role of Britain to evangelize" the world.[52] In addition, the Calvinist-political system continued under English rule. The "chosen" Governor, Assembly, and religious elders allowed prominent colonists to advise the Governor. As emigration officer, Henry's uncle, Henry Nource, would have participated in this political system.[53]

We, therefore, infer that Maynard may have internalized her father's Boer Calvinism. He was raised Calvinist, interacted with Calvinist Boers at the Cape for eighteen years, and was related to the powerful Henry Nourse. Can we further corroborate this inference from Henry's activities after the Cape? We know his success in trading commodities continued: he served as director of the London and South African Bank; had shares in numerous South African and English companies; and invested in diamonds at the Cape in 1867. In 1871, the London firm sold one of first African diamonds for £1,050.[54] We have mentioned that while philanthropical in his provision of Hawksworth cottages, a Schoolhouse, and a Hall, Henry ultimately deemed the "lower orders [like poor villagers] positively evil."[55] We may now speculate that his biases had a latent Boer-Calvinist view of "chosen." Chapter 2 addressed Henry's elitist science-religious fear that English urbanization created "feeble" paupers whose criminality, indigence, and promiscuity threatened to degenerate England's population. He believed that *all* humans were born depraved; yet his claim that the feeble were "unworthy of salvation" seemed consistent with the Boers' "intolerance" of pagan slaves "being placed on equal footing with Christians."[56]

If these were patriarchal Henry's beliefs, then how could members of his family believe differently? As we recall, most did believe differently, and they maintained their position. Louisa's wish to be buried in a simple poor person's coffin in 1878 invoked amity and respect for Hawksworth villagers. Henry's daughters Josephine and Gabrielle, who remained single, devoted their lives to village work. George would oversee the flailing family business to let Harry open his "Hope Café" in London to convert the poor. What about Constance? After visiting Scotland in 1871 she voiced repulsion toward "slothful and dirty" villagers. In 1872, she believed (like

Henry) that coal miners on strike should "be *starved* into submission!" After three years at Girton (1872–1875), she called middle-class peers shoppy or common. In 1886, she asked Westfield Council "to admit only genteel Ladies."[57] She returned from her first trip to South Africa in 1887 with not only her inflated elitism but also her innate conflation of class and race:

> What do I [Maynard] see? Ragged dirty drunken men who stumble around all over! Oh! And here at last, three women! They are shapeless bundles of black, with course black eyes. These people are disgusting! Filthy, and barefoot, and the women were shawls over their heads like dissipated looking [English] factory girls.[58]

Constance Maynard never moderated her views.

IRISHNESS AND THE PROPHET

Let us continue our story of the Maynard-Wakefield bond now that we have speculated upon the roots of Maynard's sense as prophet to see if we have altered our opinion about her (Fig. 5.3). We may detect her sense of "chosen" in her green book that suddenly resumed on 1 January 1901 after fourteen years of silence. The early green book (1866–1887) had merged piety and love feeling, and notably, it re-opened with similar outpourings: "I need only two gifts [from God] this year. One is Marion [Wakefield], and the other [evangelism] is in my hands … *May* I have them?"[59] However, Maynard now viewed evangelism though a distinct form of nationalist-imperialism. When on leave from Westfield, in 1900, her "promise" from Wakefield in Switzerland was reinforced in Egypt:

> In my [Maynard] youth I felt I would be called to be a prophet, to do some real teaching and leading of others by the power of God. I have looked in vain among English experts for that "careful walking." I heard about the new work [on Atonement theology] in Egypt, and in America. The prospect is inspiring and splendid. I feel wonderfully alone![60]

Once again, Maynard's sense of superiority was informed by her calling. God "wished [*her*] to send out Christian Ladies to evangelize the world" through a theology program (Divinity) at Westfield. Readers are somewhat condescendingly told: "M [Wakefield] is unfitted for the degree! Plans must change. I want her as my Secretary [for Divinity]."[61] But

Fig. 5.3 Constance Maynard aged fifty-six, 1905, wearing her black preaching dress with Bible in hand. Courtesy of Queen Mary University of London Archives/Westfield College/WFD. Reference WFD/1/1/5.

Maynard deemed her plans for Divinity and Wakefield noble. She had pressed Westfield Council on the matter; sought advice from various academics and theologians worldwide; persuaded OS friends to take Divinity; and had a promise from Wakefield. In fact, her green book probably resurfaced when she knew her plans were attainable. On 11 October 1901, she triumphantly announced: "Theology exists! Best of all, I have love! Can *anything* be better?" The Council "had agreed to Divinity when [she] told them that the systemic training of Scripture was considered important in the educational world." Meanwhile, Wakefield "had suddenly walked into Westfield to tell [Maynard], 'YES, I will be your Secretary for Divinity!'" Maynard added, "I *am* the new Evangelical prophet! With my faithful scribe [Wakefield] at my side, I can evangelize the world!"[62] Wakefield was to be both life partner and successor to Westfield and Divinity.

Maynard's effusive green book entries were only partly true, which recalls the ways that she constructed her life story. Certainly, she seemed truly joyful about Wakefield: "I [Maynard] am at peace. My little bed …

now sees hours of calm and content ... It is like going from midnight to a new dawn."[63] Yet her assurance that the Council-supported Divinity was disingenuous. The *Minutes* spoke only of Westfield's admission as a School of the University of London that offered a curriculum far broader than the Oxbridge Classics and Science degrees. Women could enroll in the faculties of Arts, and Law, and while excluded from Engineering, and Medicine, could take courses on Public Health and Hygiene.[64] It is notable that Maynard did not reveal the Council's true thoughts on Divinity until 1930: "They asked, '*Why* do you intend to lecture on the speculative subject of evil? We need the broader theological approach. They [students] will *not* get teaching anywhere.'"[65] This conversation absent in the green book was not recorded in the *Minutes* either, but even in October 1901, Maynard stood alone with lectures on the "unfriendly relations [evolution and religion]." The Council focused on "upgrading [Westfield's] scanty little library and laboratory [to secure its admission] as a School."[66]

Maynard's green book account of Divinity and Westfield was interesting. In chap. 4, we debated Metcalfe's and the Council's actions following Maynard's outburst at the Council meeting in 1884 because there was no evidence about what she said or did. What about the late 1890s? While the *Minutes* were silent about Divinity, we discover that Maynard sometimes disregarded the Council's concern over her lack of responsibility: she repeatedly failed to update her account book; she appointed two non-resident lecturers without first consulting the education committee, and she took a leave for nine days during the May term without the Council's consent.[67] Meanwhile, the Council's negligence of college matters is perhaps best represented by the long battle over electric lighting. The *Minutes* of 1895 suggest their half-hearted agreement to electricity even though one student nearly died from gas lamp burns. Maynard fought until 1897 to rescind switching off lights at 10:30 pm; and until 1898 to install higher wattage bulbs in rooms and even then, she had to contribute to a second light in each room because both students and staff bemoaned the lack of light.[68]

However, while colleagues appreciated Maynard's generosity, they did not always support her goals. When we return to her glowing account about Divinity in 1901 her claim, "My kindly staff leaves me to ... fight the attack on Christology and 'evil' secularism," also misled readers. In fact, some possibly colluded with the Council to forge the Classics and sciences at Westfield, for it became a School of the University in early 1902.[69] Sadly, when this happened, Divinity floundered. Fees were increased, and enrollment quickly dwindled as obdurate Maynard balked at "the align of Divinity's syllabus with that of the University of London. 'Obedience' to Christ," she believed, "should center around awful warnings and a sense of chronic anxiety."[70] Just as Calvinist Boers refuted the idea of pagan slaves on equal footing with Christians, so Maynard could not bow beneath "Romanized" Anglicanism that threatened salvation. To claim Christ as the redeemer of humankind was not the Truth of the Bible. In fact, the Incarnation directly opposed: "Forsake *all* and follow God, for He shall not forsake you."[71]

Maynard had summoned atonement theology to convey another pressing issue. Earthly treasure with Wakefield had (again) repudiated the Cloister that they now must re-enter. Maynard did not elaborate; her green book silences a stark contrast to her Hellenist and floral raptures in the late 1890s. Her self-censure may have been deliberate. We wondered at her discomfort over Amy Mantle's passion in 1875 when female friendship was a part of heteronormativity. And even in 1897, few knew Havelock Ellis's *Psychology of Sex* that classified same-sex desire as aberrant. Still, all in all, her review of 1901 was inscrutable: "Her [Wakefield's] name is not written across the year, except to say that the best of *all* earthly treasures were mine!! Yet it was not the perfect subjection and union that I had asked for and expected."[72] By February 1902, Maynard was deeply tormented by what she called,

> the inefficiency of [her] soul. I told her [Wakefield], "we need spiritual more than physical health. We must go back to the ultimate basis of our friendship. By this I mean that Love is to be second, not first, to our search for the Saviour." I said, "We must pray for resistance of the flesh, and we must fast for spiritual guidance."[73]

Not much else is written in the green book. Her diary is silent and, unfortunately, her autobiography ended when Maynard discussed the year 1901. All we know is that by late February, Wakefield's unstable struggle with living in the Cloister and sense of professional inadequacy caused another onset of acute depression. Maynard's lack of sympathy was evident: "She has evolved from being a light-hearted secretary who tends towards indolence in everything! Her Irish 'deficiencies' show failure of 'Character.'" Perhaps an angry Maynard speculated that Wakefield too had betrayed her and Divinity. Nevertheless, faith and class had bolstered Maynard's treatment of college women as "Senior" Girtonian and as

Mistress of Westfield. In this instance, Englishness continued to play a large role in her scorn of Wakefield's "slack, & forgetful, & untidy Irishness." These failings had caused Wakefield to lose her missionary spirit.[74]

Certainly, we might be tempted to argue that Maynard's egoistic piety caused an unhealthy and perverse social relationship on a personal level. Even so, we must consider her faith- and empire-minded actions in historical context. Let us investigate how fin de siècle norms shaped Maynard's attitudes and Wakefield's reaction to them. We discover that women's demand for higher education had caused a backlash. Society greatly feared the breakdown of female domestic piety that threatened "Englishness" and its cultivating morality. Maynard's disgust at Wakefield's Irish deficiencies attested to English views of the Irish as "slack and sloppy." Evolutionists like Darwin and Huxley maintained their "proof" that the English were the most evolved species of the ape. At the bottom lay "pagan sub-species" like African native tribes, who were ancestors of "cruel, and torturing savages." They also claimed that their theories on "English progress and civilization [that subordinated the Irish] were sound, and ethical." In short, Wakefield's genetic deficiencies caused the failure of character.[75]

Of course, there were scientists who challenged Darwin's and others' views. As Alfred Wallace claimed: "The more I see of 'uncivilized' people, the better I think of human nature on the whole. [In fact], the essential differences between so-called civilized and savage man seem to disappear." As for Ireland, he added, "the results of British domination have been rebellion, famine, and depopulation—these must be surely reckoned among the most terrible and most disastrous failure of the Nineteenth Century."[76] Whether Wakefield would have agreed with Wallace or not, new scientific ideas certainly helped her to contend with Maynard's accusations. She sought a physician who "alarmed by [her] low pulse and low weight, diagnosed [her] with neurasthenia." She told Maynard that pressure to become the future leader of Divinity had caused her stress. How did Maynard react? She with great relief assured readers that "M's neurasthenia [was] *not* complicated by hysteria [female madness]!"[77] If society struggled with religious doubt, Wakefield's battle between faith and science was not unusual. Here, we have another example of how Maynard chose to confront her mistake by directing blame towards the cultural climate.

However, another green book entry belied Wakefield's science–faith conflict. Although she was to undergo the well-known "Cure" of bedrest and overfeeding, many doctors now deemed the Cure harmful because anxiety was a mental rather than physiological or spiritual crisis.[78] Meanwhile, Maynard's guilt-ridden reaction was as clear in her diary: "Dinner is a pitiful sight. This is not for M at all. She must leave!" In fact, when removing Wakefield from her Cure, Maynard offered Wakefield an escape from their relationship: "I told her, 'I *do* leave you free.'" But apparently, Wakefield teasingly kissed Maynard saying, "free for this?" Maynard "felt as desperate for kissing!"[79] Whether the incident happened, or was aberrant, or typical, the green book implied they were lovers.

When Wakefield decided to return to Westfield in October 1904, Maynard expected their passionate encounters to continue. Wakefield, however, had other romantic plans: "She [Wakefield] resolutely shuts her door at night," Maynard lamented. In late October, Wakefield tersely told Maynard: "My love for [new student] Mary [Armitage] is a whole new experience. I am leaving Westfield." She left Maynard for the final time.[80] Divinity struggled on at Maynard's expense until 1908, at which time Maynard shrank back into a secularist Westfield that flourished as a School of the University of London. She bemoaned "the loss of Wakefield's full lips" and Westfield's "cultivating spirit" until she retired in 1913. For her part, Wakefield declared that leaving Maynard "had opened a new life." She enrolled in Bedford College in 1910 and would graduate with a BA in Philosophy. She would then complete an MA in Philosophy (that intersected with the new field of Psychology) and establish a teaching career.[81]

....

We may not accept but we now better understand Maynard's colonial affairs. We may not condone her inability to moderate her views of "otherness" about those unlike herself. But this does not suggest that Maynard was oblivious to her biases or felt trouble-free. We will return to the extraordinary aftermath of the Maynard–Wakefield bond in our concluding chapter. Of course, whether we will resolve our unanswered questions about Maynard's mistakes is doubtful. We cannot authenticate the past when we were not there. Nor can we assume our grasp of the nuances of historical change. Consider, for example, the divergence between Maynard and the Council over Westfield's goals and the Divinity program. We might sympathize with the Council's timely professionalization of Westfield. To them, Maynard's faith-based approach to higher education was outmoded and possibly, threatened Westfield's academic reputation.

Nevertheless, our sympathy with the Council may result from presentist views; especially if we dismiss Maynard's credence to "the stern literal views of Evangelical fathers." After all, with "modern learning on one hand, and the Bible on the other," she bravely sought to alter late-Victorian views on femininity and women's economic independence. As she explained, if the Bible "br[ought] the *whole* of human nature together," society should consider education as important for women as it was for men.[82] Late-Victorian attitudes did not change, and women today still fight for workplace rights. Thus, Maynard was far from "wrong" or meek or conservative in her promotion of moral Character globally. This is how she subverted the Victorian construct of femininity. As for sexual feelings, Maynard would have to face it head-on during her retirement years

Notes

1. *Budget* IV, Sept 2, 1903.
2. *A*, VII, 60, "October Term 1897," 400, written in 1928. In 1895, out of the twelve B.A. candidates, seven gained a First Class while only two failed (*Minutes*, 2 May 1894, 77 and 4 December 1895, 99).
3. Beatrice Cadbury to Janet Sondheimer, April 1974, Ms. 213 Special Collections, Courtesy of Queen Mary University of London Archives/ Westfield/ College/WFD).
4. *D*, 8 October 1897, 87. For the Imperial Federal League see Porter, "Empire and World," 159.
5. Irene Biss, *Reminiscences, 1907–1911* (London: Hodder, 1921); and *D*, 12 December 1902, 24.
6. Firth, *Constance Louisa Maynard*, 39–55; *A*, IV, 27, "1876, At home," 58–59, written in 1925.
7. The epitome of British empire in South Africa followed British annexation of Natalia (1848) and the second South Africa War. Though the British swiftly occupied the Boer republics, the Boers refused to accept defeat and engaged in guerrilla warfare. The British brought the remaining Boer guerrillas to the negotiating table which ended the war (see Porter, *Religion and Empire*, 45–60).
8. *Travel Diary, 1886, 3–4*; and Constance Louisa Maynard, "A Nation of Children, or Impressions of a Fortnight in Pondoland," *The South African Pioneer* (1897), 10, 152.
9. Brian Howard Harrison, *Peaceable Kingdom: Stability and Change in Modern Britain* (Oxford: Oxford University Press, 1982), 138.
10. For Henry, see *D*, 4 May 1871, 2. For more on Malthus and science see Bratlinger, *Dark Vanishing*, 164, 188.

11. Herbert Spencer, *The Study of Sociology* 6*th* ed., (London: Henry S. King & Co, 1877), 188. See also Newsome, *Victorian World, 157–158;* and Bratlinger, *Dark Vanishings*, 178.
12. Alfred Russel Wallace, *Wonderful Century: Its Success and Failures* (London: S. Sonnenschein 1898), 372.
13. The S.V.M.U. sent guest speakers to Westfield on a regular basis (*D*, 6 January 1900, 54; 4 May 1902, 99; and 9 October 1904, 231).
14. *D*, 31 December 1904, 365. For Biblical Criticism see, for example, Riesen, *Criticism and Faith*.
15. *A*, VII, "Thüringen Wald, 1897," 407, written in 1929. When the leader of spiritual activities cancelled, Westfield colleague Anne Richardson proposed her "young, pleasant cousin [Marion]."
16. *Travel Diary*, 1900, 2; and *D*, 6 September 1872, 22. For Ireland see, Heyck and Veldman, *Peoples of British Isles*, 454, 475–476.
17. Walter L. Arnstein, *Britain Yesterday and Today: 1830 to the Present 8th ed.*, (Boston: Houghton Mifflin, 2002), 171. Ireland became a critical context for debates between Irish Catholics and Presbyterians and between Anglo-Irish and English on how Irishness was to be defined and related to England.
18. *A*, VII, "Thüringen Wald 1897," 401, 411, written in 1929. Copied from *GB*, May 1897.
19. *D*, 26 June 1872, 111, 116; and *A*, III, 26, "My last Term at Girton, 1875," 699, written in 1918.
20. See *D*, 26 June 1872, 111, 116.
21. Sharon Marcus, *Between Women: Friendship, Desire and Marriage in Victorian England* (New York: Basic Books, 2007), 109–149.
22. For Harrison, see Yopie Prins, "Greek Maenads, Victorian Spinsters," in *Victorian Sexual Dissidence*, ed., Richard Dellamora (Chicago: The University of Chicago Press, (1999), 43–81. In *Same-Sex Desire in Victorian Religious Culture* (Basingstoke: Palgrave Macmillan, (2002), 48, 67, 83, Frederick Roden analyzed how individuals among them, Christina Rosetti, subverted heteronormative culture by depicting a "queer" non-phallic Christ and sexually charged all-female communities. See also Ruth Vanita, *Sappho, and the Virgin Mary: Same-Sex Love and the English Literary Imagination* (New York: Columbus University Press, 1996).
23. *A*, VII, 59, "1897," 411, written in 1928. For philosophical thinking see Heyck, *Intellectual Life*, 190–195; and for sexualities see Beasley, *Gender & Sexuality*, 117–127.
24. See Smith, *Between Mind and Nature*, 40–42, 45–46.
25. See *A*, VII, 61, "May Term 1898," 411, written in 1929.
26. *A*, VII, 63, "May Term 1899," 444, written in 1929.
27. *A*, VII, 62, "October Term 1898," 430, written in 1929.

28. *GB,* 20 December 1904, 66.
29. See Vicinus, *Intimate Friends,* xx, 98–108.
30. See Anna Clark, "Twilight Moments," *Journal of the History of Sexuality,* 14, 1/2 (2005), 140,152. See also Wilson, *History In Crisis?* 117–118; and Popkin, *Herodotus to H-Net,* 133–140.
31. *Budget* III 1899; and V, 1900.
32. *A,* VII, 64, "Egypt, 1900," 454, written in 1929.
33. See Doan, *Disturbing Practices;* and Beasley, *Gender & Sexuality,* 123–124.
34. For pioneer work in the field, see Barbara N. Ramusack, "Embattled Advocates: The Debate over Birth Control in India 1920–1940," *Journal of Women's History* 1, 2, (1989) 34–64. For later work see, Nupur Chaudhuri and Margaret Strobel, eds., *Western Women and Imperialism: Complicity and Resistance* (Bloomington: Indiana University Press, 1992); Phillipa Levine, ed., *Gender and Empire* (Oxford: Oxford University Press, 2007); and Ann Laura Stoler, *Carnal Knowledge,* 32–34.
35. One exception is Naomi Lloyd's "Religion, Same-Sex Desire, and the Imagined Geographies of Empire: The Case of Constance Maynard," *Women's History Review* 25, 1, (2016), 53–73, which analyzes how religion informed the empire-minded informed Maynard's erotic positioning of Wakefield.
36. For more on the development of the fields of empire and postcolonialism see Camiscioli, "Gender, Intimacy, and Empire," 138–148.
37. R.G. Collingwood, *The Idea of History* (Oxford; Clarendon Press, 1946), 257. For Maynard's thought on her mother, see, for example, *GB,* 3 August 1873, 111; and 8 October 1882, 149.
38. Firth, *Constance Louisa Maynard,* 20, 29.
39. For Henry's discussion about "prophets" see, for example, *GB,* 12 June 1867, 120; 3 October 1867, 139; and 3 December 1869, 7.
40. For Ginzburg see Wilson, *History in Crisis?* 75–76.
41. *A,* III, 11, "Girton, 1872," 355, written in 1919.
42. *GB,* 12 June 1867, 120; and 3 December 1869, 7. There is little written about the late Erskine's Scottish friend and "live prophet," the Reverend John Macleod Campbell, whom both Henry and Constance met in Scotland in 1871. But Campbell "caught [Constance's] *inmost* thought when he prayed that [they] might bring forth fruit unto God. He inspired Westfield's motto based upon Irving's *Sower:* "God's Word on an open heart brings forth fruit. Let the inner life be greater than the worldly."
43. For more Calvinism and Erskine see Bebington, *Evangelicalism in Modern Britain,* 22–40.
44. Firth, *Constance Louisa Maynard,* 38–39. For Cape empire see Nanni Giordano, *The Colonisation of Time* (Manchester: Manchester University Press, 2012).

45. Firth, *Constance Louisa Maynard*, 39–55; and *A*, IV, 27, "1876, At home," 58–59, written in 1925.
46. Thomas Baines, *Exploration in South Africa* (London: Langham Green 1861).
47. Alan Cohen, "Mary Elizabeth Barber [ne Bowker], Some Early South African Geologists, and the Discovery of Diamonds," *Earth Sciences History*, V. 22, 2, (2003), 156–171.
48. André Du Toit, "No Chosen People: The Myth of the Calvinist Origins of Afrikaner Nationalism and Racial Ideology," *The American Historical Review* 88, 4 (1983), 927.
49. *D*, 31 December 1904, 365. For Biblical Criticism see, for example, Riesen, *Criticism and Faith*.
50. See Antoinette Burton and Tony Ballantyne, "Introduction: Bodies, Empires, and World Histories," in Burton and Ballantyne eds., *Bodies in Contact: Rethinking Colonial Encounter in World History*, (Durham: Duke University Press, 2005), 3. For recent work on the idea of multiple compound identities see, for example, Anne Laura Stoler, *Duress: Imperial Studies in Our Times*, (Durham: Duke University Press, 2016); and Sarah Curtiss, *Civilizing Habits: Women Missionaries and the Revival of French Empire* (Oxford: Oxford University Press, 2012).
51. In "From Apartheid to Liberation: Calvinism and the Shaping of Ethical Belief in South Africa" *Sociological Focus*, 24, 2, (1991), 129–143, Timothy M. Renick notes that theological symbols which guided and grounded the Boers continue within a radically new South African society.
52. Nile Green, "Parnassus of the Evangelical Empire: Orientalism and the English Universities, 1800–50," *The Journal of Imperial and Commonwealth History* 40, 3, (2013), 337–355. See also Du Toit, "Chosen Peoples," 29–31; and Porter, "Empire and World", 144.
53. Nourse oversaw the largest emigration scheme in 1820 (King, *Reminiscences*, 30–31).
54. The discovery of diamonds by the Orange river in the Transvaal in 1867 culminated in the British Union of South Africa in 1910. Because digging for diamonds was expensive, only the wealthy like Henry could support themselves and trade overseas (The Reverend Dr. Williams, Dean of Grahamstown, in "New South African Diamond Fields," *The Yearbook of Facts, 1866*, 202–209).
55. *D*, 3 August 1871, 80; and Firth, *Constance Louisa Maynard*, 38–42.
56. See *GB*, February 12, 1868, 69; and *D*, 4 May 1871 2.
57. See *D*, 3 July 1871, 23; 12 May 1875, 99; and 6 March 1886, 122.
58. *Travel Diary*, 1886.
59. *GB*, 1 January 1901, 1.

60. *GB*, 1 January 1901, 1; and *A*, VII, 64, "Egypt, 1900," 455, written in January 1930.
61. *GB*, 1 January 1901, 1.
62. *GB*, 12 October 1901, 67.
63. *GB*, 15 October 1901, 69.
64. Compare *GB*, 11 May 1901, 25–26, with *Minutes*, 12 May 1901, 74.
65. *A*, VII, 66, "October Term 1901," 470, written in March 1930.
66. Compare *A*, VII, 66, "October Term 1901," 478–480, written in March 1930, with *Minutes*, 12 June 1901, 680.
67. Compare *Minutes*, 8 November 1897, 265, with *D*, 13 October 1897, 77.
68. See *Minutes*, 7 June 1898, 312; and 19 September 1900, 42, and compare with *GB*, 13 October 1897, 77.
69. Compare *A*, VII, 66, "October Term 1901," 478–480, written in March 1930, with Firth, *Constance Louisa Maynard*, 287–309.
70. *GB*, 19 February 1902, 140.
71. See *GB*, 29 December 1901, 117——she had noted similar sentiments in May 1886, 146——and compare with Du Toit, "Chosen Peoples," 23.
72. *GB*, 31 December 1901, 98.
73. *GB*, 19 February 1902, 100.
74. *GB*, 24 February 1902, 113.
75. *GB*, 24 February 1902, 113. For backlash against women's higher learning see Carstens, "Unbecoming Women." For the Irish see Newsome, *World Picture*, 128–129; and for social Darwinism see Bratlinger, *Dark Vanishings*, 172–176.
76. Wallace, *Wonderful Century*, 375.
77. *GB*, 19 February 1902, 110–112.
78. *GB*, 20 February 1902, 117. For changing opinion on piety and physiological conditions, see Janet Oppenheim, *Shattered Nerves: Doctors, Patients, and Depression in Victorian England* (New York: Oxford University Press, 1991).
79. See *D*, 7 May 1902, 89; *GB*, April 1902, 12; and 20 May 1902, 116.
80. *GB*, 22 October 1904, 267. Armitage, granddaughter of Canon Gibbon, remained with Wakefield until 1907.
81. See *GB*, 25 March 1908, 10; and 31 October 1908, 168. For Wakefield see Vicky Holmes, College Archivist, to Pauline Phipps, 17 December 2010.
82. See *GB*, 12 October 1901, 67; and Maynard, *We Women*, 130–132. Quote modified from Gal. III: 28, 657. See also, Bebbington, *Evangelicalism*, 181–190; and for women's agency from religion see deVries, "More than Paradoxes to Offer: Feminism, History and Religious Cultures," in *Women, Gender, and Religious Cultures in Britain, 1800–1940*, eds., deVries and Morgan, (London: Routledge, 2010), 188–210.

CHAPTER 6

"Noisy Rabble of Our Fears," 1917–1934

Abstract The elderly Maynard floundered under innovative theories of the psyche that infiltrated Britain in the mid-1920s. She was particularly troubled by the new idea that a sexually repressed childhood like hers could, in later life, lead the individual to seek abnormal outlets for their excessively strong sexual excitations. This chapter outlines Maynard's painful reconsideration of what she now called her misuse of love when her former lover, the Irish Marion Wakefield, became a pioneer student of psychology and, later, psychoanalysis. Virtually nothing is written on late-Victorian women who not only pioneered in studies on the psyche, but lived through vast changes in the field. Maynard left behind only brief thoughts on her Girton studies and conversations about psychology and psychoanalysis with Wakefield in 1917, 1923, and 1934. Nonetheless, her memoirs convey two late-Victorian women's astonishing reflections on their intimate past due to their unique expertise in psychology.

Keywords Singularization of History • Psychology • Psychoanalysis • Ownership • Textual Environment

© The Author(s), under exclusive license to Springer Nature Switzerland AG 2023
P. A. Phipps, *A Victorian Educational Pioneer's Evangelicalism, Leadership, and Love*,
https://doi.org/10.1007/978-3-031-13999-4_6

At age fifty-five, Maynard spoke her mind about a burgeoning scientific field:

> To have religion with its most intimate secrets, all handled from the psychologist's point of view is nothing short of outstanding; but the idea is dangerous—WE control our bodies—which of course is poison to Christianity…The enemy [secularism] has not gone but has changed shape. Evil is real and frightfully strong, but our wills can come over to God's side and control the noisy rabble of our fears.[1]

Her newsletter to former Westfield students (OS) in 1904 waxed bittersweet about the "new psychology." An OS had recommended William James's revolutionary *Varieties of Religious Experience* (1902) that scientifically defined religious attitudes. As a pioneer of psychology, James's research into thought processes led him to ask: Why are Christians as convinced by "unseen reality" as by "direct" life experiences?[2] *Religious Experience* captivated yet disturbed Maynard. As it was, she agonized over Marion Wakefield's flight from Westfield for worldly love (Mary Armitage). Now, James insinuated that belief in a "*God* who guided Will" was not only misguided but erroneous.[3] Maynard's ambivalence over James's psychology likely prompted painful Girton memories of Jeremy Bentham's assertion: "humans create their *own* beliefs and then act upon them. [Bentham's] very idea [did after all] plague [Maynard] for the rest of [her] life."[4] Shortly before she died, Maynard confessed that her "biggest mistake in life was cho[osing] human love over divine love."[5] However, as we know, science from her Tripos had impelled her distinct successes and emotional longings in extraordinary ways.

This chapter continues Maynard's story (as we have) by establishing facts and interpreting them through methods that tie to microhistory. But what if facts change? In 1926, Maynard aged seventy-seven voiced shock and "abhorrence at the new psychoanalysis" that classified intimate female–female ties, "abnormal sex feeling."[6] Her disquiet seemed valid, for her diaries never discussed Havelock Ellis, or sexology, and in 1917, only briefly mentioned psychology. However, when I discovered she had read James's *Religious Experience* in 1904, my opinion altered, for she knew more about developments in psychology than her diaries and autobiography claimed. Maynard's newsletter was for this historian a crucial find. It not only changed the central argument for this chapter, it reaffirmed my speculation about the impact of Maynard's Tripos upon her life. What about her disgust of psychoanalysis? Certainly, confronting this new psychological theory would have forced her (as many others) to re-think same-sex intimacy. As the historian Roger Smith explains, Freud unlike other psychologists "emphasized sex at the expense of all else."[7] However, Freud published his first major work in 1905. The question is, *did* Maynard first learn of psychoanalysis in 1926? If it was earlier than she admitted, how did it impact her life?

We have discussed how research can be a serendipitous process, especially when exciting new insights remind us that history is never complete.[8] In this, and perhaps more fortuitous than my discovery of Maynard's newsletter, was unearthing Wakefield's "voice" that had to this point been silent. Maynard's green book sporadically relayed how Wakefield as a pioneer student of psychology had in 1917 completed an MA. Her snipes about Wakefield's studies seemed useful upshots of their ongoing hostilities; that is, until I located Wakefield's MA and discovered morbid characterizations of Maynard and their relations; characterizations that invoked psychoanalytical language. I wondered (once again) if Maynard knew of psychoanalysis before 1926. "Noisy Rabble" opens with Maynard's reaction to James and life in early retirement to see if her preconceptions about worldliness and faith changed. We then turn to conversations between Maynard and Wakefield in 1917, 1923, and 1934 to highlight two late-Victorian women's extraordinary knowledge of new psychological theories that dramatically altered their views on their past intimacy.

William James's Noisy Rabble

Overall, as a pioneer of the Mental and Moral Tripos, the pious Maynard could not help but appraise James's notion of self-determination "nothing short of outstanding." After all, he deemed the "spiritual self ... more self-satisfying than the social and material selves."[9] James's innovative concept of "selves" of course, bespoke his elite, religious, scientific, and consumerist society, just as ideas of class, faith, science, femininity, and empire-influenced Maynard.[10] Nevertheless, his theories provoked her excruciating life-long conflict. While her newsletter of 1904 condemned his "new psychology for poison[ing] Christianity," another in 1906 declared "the idea of 'mental healing' lovely!"[11] Meanwhile, a diary entry in 1906 that exclaimed, "I am ever in awe over the metaphysical concept 'being,'" implied the ways in which her Tripos had fueled her self-expression of leadership, love, and choice.[12] This noted, Maynard's mull over her mistakes had often culminated with: "'Will' not given to God is 'evil.'" Her newsletter similarly warned OS that any thought of human agency was dangerous. James's *Religious Experience* only "proved that the 'enemy' ha[d] ... changed shape. Evil [was] frightfully strong, but if we sought God, we could control the 'noisy rabble of our fears.'"[13]

As we might expect, Maynard also blamed the noisy rabble for Divinity's failure in 1904. In her view, the lack of support for theology was a sign of the emergent psychological times,

> The Age of Authority is gone, I [Maynard] fear; indeed, it is long over. The High [Anglican] Church offers its wares so much cheaper: discipline, self-denial, and assurance—all are prices we can pay without touching our inner soul. But the Bible shews new philosophies of Science were foretold as subtle temptations from Satan.[14]

Her reaction was telling. Divinity had fallen because the cheaper wares of incarnational theology and secularist thinking tempted Westfield as a School of the University. She was, however, relieved that the enemy had not completely engulfed Britain: "England need[ed] a revival like that in Wales [Britain]." Maynard referred to an obscure yet huge Welsh Christian revival (1904–1905); a "resistance" that, notably linked to Calvinism, emphasized "eternal torment" followed those who did not atone for earthliness. As an individual criticized for her outmoded beliefs by Westfield Council, colleagues, and college loves Maynard proudly acclaimed herself "a part of this resistance."[15]

The "Age of Authority" in England persisted despite the rise of secularism. Maynard anticipated the yearly Churchman's Conference "where eminent clergyman defended the Gospels." She as we know fashioned (through prophet Isaiah) a "suffering (Calvinist) elect" that aimed to "evangelize the increasingly secularist world." Her fight against "careless Agnosticism" continued after her retirement in 1913. Her various published books, articles, and tracts on worldliness would have likely seemed conservative to most. *The Prophet Daniel* (1914) particularly symbolized her life-long "sacrifice of Will" to God. In her view, "modern faith that emphasized morality was *NO* effort of Will ... in God's eyes."[16] Yet her plea did, in fact, reflect cultural scissions during a time of crisis in faith. The split of evangelicalism over atonement-thinking and incarnational Christology had caused acute societal unrest that, in part, explained the failure of Maynard's Divinity program by 1904. Nonetheless, hundreds of Westfield graduates rose above Evangelical disjuncture to "normalize" female missionary work at home and overseas. Religion, when combined with women's fight for education rights, was a platform for action and change as women increasingly entered professionalism to gain independence.[17]

Still, while she claimed to be a part of the resistance, Maynard failed to resist the noisy rabble. In 1905, a year after she read James, she became obsessed with the first exponent of German idealism, Johann Gottlieb Fichte, who was deemed as influential as Immanuel Kant. Her essay, "Five Levels of Life," incorporated Fichte's "planes of life" such as ambition, self-control, and altruism, but then admitted her inability to reach the last plane, whereby the Christian relinquished will to God: "A passionate nature makes it almost *impossible* to choose the Cloister. Mentally I [Maynard] chose it, but not my heart, and the retrospect is sad."[18] For Maynard, dedication to the cause and emotional longings were barriers to the fifth level. Perhaps this explains why she was so committed to Divinity at Westfield.

Maynard continued to balance life interests, longing, and faith during her retirement years. Certainly, we discover the impediments and trials of old age: rotten teeth, gout, shingles, painful rheumatism, and a weak heart. We also learn of loss: from the passing of family like her sister Josephine (1907), to the strife between Harry and George over business that remained unresolved at Harry's death in 1918. But Maynard's unceasing energy was as evident in her cycling across England and Scotland to see friends until her mid-seventies. Meanwhile, her green book captured cultural change or "great waves of thought" when she delivered guest lectures at Westfield: "'Life!' it's 'always interesting!' I deal with education, England, and the world (the awakening of India and China);" and again: "We *must* accept the Zeitgeist [spirit of the age] for the seed comes from God."[19] Her newsletter and diary, in turn, effused patriotic religiosity: "Female missionaries make us proud! Wherever England comes, law and order begin;"[20] and about World War I: "I look at men dressed in khaki and think how their bodies might be maimed or killed! But then again, I think, yes, England is worth such lives."[21] When Maynard spoke about science, however, she verged between awe and fear:

> Mathematics, Philosophy, History, and Language has placed in our very hands the *best* thoughts through past ages, and therefore we *rightly* stand at the summit of all kinds of knowledge ... But is there no danger to this?... Have we not heard of devoted scientific thinkers making shipwreck of their faith? Yes, we admit it, there is danger, very great danger.[22]

Fig. 6.1 Westfield College (at Kidderpore) Dining Hall, undated. Courtesy of Queen Mary University of London Archives/Westfield College/WFD. Reference WFD/12/10/1.

James's *Religious Experience* was dangerous and evil, Maynard fumed, because such noisy rabble had destroyed the Cloister; abstinence that *she* avoided due to scientific aim, professionalism, and sexual longings. Let us explore why she struggled so much (Figs. 6.1 and 6.2).

The Singularization of History

Throughout this book, our interpretation of small events caused by Maynard's "Cloister" and ambition uncovered layers of overt biases: Maynard's, the Council's, and Victorians' thoughts on women's higher education, professionalism, and empire; Maynard's and Victorians crisis in faith from new science; and Maynard's and Victorians views on female–female intimacy. We also uncovered covert layers of biases: in Maynard's dissonant archival voices; in how she chose to reflect on her life; and the ways that she confronted her mistakes. Meanwhile, this historian's biases took form as she constructed Maynard's story, unraveled Maynard's narrative(s); and analyzed events that shaped Maynard's mistakes. Readers

Fig. 6.2 Students in attic Laboratory, Westfield College (at Kidderpore), c. 1916. Courtesy of Queen Mary University of London Archives/Westfield College/WFD. Reference WFD/25/4/2.

have undoubtedly read this book with their own biases. Still, these layers of biases laid bare extraordinary knowledge about Maynard's thought processes.

Considering this, Sigurður Gylfi Magnússon's micro-historical "singularization of history" in a sense, follows R.G. Collingwood's view that facts are useful to uncover the workings of past mindsets. Magnússon argues that the tiny event or singular thinking does not have to correspond to the structural whole; indeed, the tiny can reveal flaws in the so-called metanarrative. He applied his method to uncover, for example,

Icelandic peasants' thoughts on life and death. He first included a discussion of macro-level investigations that, based upon statistics, argued that Icelandic rural life between the late 1800s and early 1900s was one of steady progress. When he compared these findings with writing by rural people themselves, a vastly different picture emerged. It was a time when Icelanders felt pessimistic, even hopeless. Certainly, Magnússon believes it useful to tie the micro to the macro. However, in his view, the microhistorian's task is to dig deeper into mindsets of individuals who endured an experience or event.[23]

We may view Magnússon's approach to microhistory postmodernist in his skepticism about "objective macro knowledge." When Hayden White published *Metahistory* in 1973, he challenged language as a neutral medium in history writing. Meanwhile, in *Discipline and Punish* (1975), Michel Foucault proposed that "metanarratives were contrived by scholars" rather than accurate depictions. The emergence of postmodernist theory in the 1970s thus, worked in tandem with the linguistic turn to challenge assumptions about the "truth" of any discourse. Historians rejected single explanations about the past, linear stories about events, and the idea of history as "complete." The postmodernist-based queer theory in the 1990s found form in studies on gender, sexuality, race, and empire (i.e., deconstructing the binary metropole/colony).[24]

We have explored how a conservative pious elite white woman's self-reflections relayed the incongruity between her familial upbringing and cultural ideals about femininity, class, sexuality, and faith. In short, Maynard's experiences invoked "the instability" of identity formation while her expressions of love exampled the "multiplicity and fluidity" of the self. The nuances of clue finding and the concept of mentalité also greatly helped our queer analysis of Maynard's "mistakes." Certainly, obscure comments, tropes, and figurative language restricted our interpretation of her acts, but queering her archive proffered tenable verdicts on her mentalité. For example, when we considered how she thought rather than judging what she did. This has been the case when we followed clues and puzzles. In Chap. 2, we questioned if a fact could ever *not* be a fact.

In this, Magnússon conceives an individual's "textual environment" (diaries, letters, or poems) as circumstantial traces, rather than mirror images of past reality. He does not suggest that a past mindset is inaccessible to historians. Historians write history based on evidence, and usually believe their history is valid, which is why they write them in the first place. To Magnússon, carefully examined traces of evidence about a past can become facts that are as important as any concrete statement they may make.[25] As an elderly woman, living in the early 1900s, Maynard often avoided speaking about emotions. But when she did, it was fascinating. She not only understood feeling through faith and late-Victorian culture, she alluded to past sexual struggles through the new psychological language.

So, now that we have introduced our methods section, let us continue Maynard's tale. Our queer singularization of her life is a sad, though provocative one. We will re-consider etymology and structural semantics in our close examination of her recorded interactions with Wakefield. Our aim is to display how fascinating traces of evidence about tiny events illuminate profound changes in ideas about sexuality, which classified heterosexuality in opposition to all other "abnormal" sex. Indeed, we discover that the elderly Maynard had a remarkable clarity of vision when writing about her past.

"MISUSE OF PASSION" AND "HUMILIATION"

In 1906, two years after Wakefield had left Westfield with Mary Armitage, Maynard told readers without explanation: "I am not jealous but upset that M [Marion] has handed what I gave her to Mary ... When M wanted to express love she knew no language but what I had taught her."[26] Since Maynard still avoided explanation on "love" and possibly sex feeings, we might suppose that Wakefield conceived love for Armitage within the context of Maynard's floral-religious language. The elderly Maynard's cogitations about love and sex while veiled, and intermittent, disclosed more about her past. In 1910, when Wakefield enrolled in philosophy at Bedford College, London, Maynard feared that

> [Wakefield] was in a worldly, frivolous atmosphere. She only spoke about dress, men, and marriage. I [Maynard] know the usual feelings *were* missed out of her life and given to me. And what do I see and fear from this lack in her life? This abstinence, which is now revenging itself. Her Evangelical instincts are quite lost.[27]

Their mutual same-sex desire, Maynard sadly confessed, had diverted Wakefield from usual heterosexual feelings. She had forced abstinence upon Wakefield who was now "revenging" through a worldly interest in science, fashion, and men. Secularism had taken precedence over evangelizing, and Maynard felt deep remorse. She was to blame.

A green book passage seven years later, in 1917, invoked even more astonishing insight into Maynard's deep regret over "past mistakes" with Wakefield. We first learn that Wakefield had gained degrees in philosophy from Bedford College (1913) and Royal Holloway College (1917). Maynard then told readers that she "felt saddened—indeed, *mortified*," because Wakefield's MA reflected the new field of psychology. We recall that at Girton, Maynard studied writers who did not yet refer to psychology, even though they analyzed such individual capacities as motivation. However, Wakefield wrote her MA as psychology emerged as a new discipline, and Wakefield, it seems, wanted Maynard to confront their past and her Tripos.[28] Maynard's faith-flora-introspection was telling: "When I *think* of what we had, I feel humiliated. I *misused* passion. I made the white roses sent to me flush with threads in the heart." She continued,

> Yet if M were still the same, I would still love her; the skin, the tall frame, the splendid thick hair, the full lips, and the white teeth—all are only grievance landmarks of what is lost. I believe the "real bond" *was* spiritual. She did not know that it was a treasure that she would never find again. I give thanks for what she once was, but she can't do that.[29]

This neatly penciled passage startled, nestled as it was beside seemingly everyday remarks. Maynard's choice of vocabulary, diction, and sentence structure warrants further dismantling and inspection. In "Colonial Affairs," we noted that in the late 1890s a few bold late-Victorian women adapted floral language like bloom to characterize female genitalia. We wondered if Maynard's allusion to coloring Wakefield's "snowy bloom" red implied that she and Wakefield engaged in sex acts, or whether it was a narrow reading.[30] Writing in 1917, the sixty-eight-year-old Maynard romanticized Wakefield's physical beauty. She still claimed to have "made [Wakefield's] white roses flush with threads of the heart," but now introduced the term "misuse," to explain her overall treatment of Wakefield. In 1906, Maynard assured readers that she was *not* jealous but upset that Wakefield shared their language with another love. Now, in 1917, she effused a kaleidoscope of emotions: irritation, loss, and guilt over their past. Was she still mostly concerned by Wakefield's sinful turn to secularism?

Perhaps. But let us re-examine her confession in 1910: "The usual feelings *were* missed out of [Wakefield's] life and given to me." Did Maynard now think her passion with Wakefield in the late 1890s had been unusual? If so, why? Passion among pious women was still a part of heteronormative culture. Might we surmise that James, Fichte, and particularly

Wakefield impelled Maynard to re-think her faith? What about Maynard's "humiliation" over "misuse [of] passion" seven years later in 1917? Certainly, we might interpret her behavior as sexual exploitation, but that would be limiting as well as presentist. For her part, while clearly shameful over coloring Wakefield's "white rose red," Maynard quickly assured readers: "I believe the 'real bond' *was* spiritual."[31] After all, she had adopted variations of secularist-religious discourses to justify desire. In 1866: "You *may* feel God's presence in your *weakness* upon His love, but you may be treating Him like an earthly lover!"; in 1871: "It is as if we [Maynard and Hetty Lawrence] both hold the end of electric chains and sparks exchange between us, only *I* know I am holding God"; in 1874: "Amy [Mantle] *needs* to kiss me … before she resists the human flame and finds God;" and in 1897, "The colours grew brilliant as I thought of [love], [but] all the while Christ stood beside me, offering me white, pure white."[32]

It *seems* that Maynard was not cognizant of "misusing" college loves until the 1900s. We cannot thus determine whether her renunciation of desire for herself and her loves was a pleasurable part of Maynard's sexuality. Therefore, it remains difficult for the historian to ascertain whether faith was a shield rather than a belief to explain her actions. To classify or compress her carnal behaviors, as some present-day scholars might, does not seem useful.[33] Queering her languages of love has allowed us a more fluid space to conceive her distinct self-identities. For example, although she was ascetic, her Tripos inspired her to express intense (possibly sexual) feelings in unusual and powerful ways. But let us pause on her Tripos, for as implied above, there seemed to have been dramatic changes in studies on the mental. In fact, historians of science identify a slow transition between 1875 and 1925, which involved the shift from a philosophical debate on human nature to "psychology" as a coherent individuated scientific discourse. In other words, from a discussion on developments of the normal human psyche to concern about pathologies of the mind, conduct, and its consequences.[34] As Maynard herself may well have explained, from John Locke's reassuring vision of ideas derived from sensation and experience, towards focus on an individual's "misuse" of others and ensuing humiliation about it.

"HUMILIATION" AND "OWNERSHIP"

We may further dismantle Maynard's humiliation while keeping in mind Michel Foucault's postmodernist warning in *Discipline and Punish*: "Historians engage in the exercise of power" by choosing what counts as evidence.[35] Our analysis of Maynard's humiliation is inevitably biased, but it is nonetheless based upon evidence we have collected. We know that class influenced Maynard's bond with Mantle, and that Maynard's Englishness impacted Wakefield. We might ask, did Maynard's shame over "misuse" also infer her superior minded "conquest" of Wakefield?

In "Colonial Affairs," we explored Maynard's acts of dominance over Wakefield's Irishness. She hoped that the pious Wakefield would succeed her as Mistress, but when Wakefield "failed" her, Maynard reduced Wakefield's indolence as "proof" of her Irish failings. Did Maynard now feel guilt over using Irishness to criticize Wakefield? What about Wakefield's emotional breakdowns themselves? Were they not faith- and sex-based? In 1902, Maynard rejoiced over Wakefield's "respectable" neurasthenia that "was *not* complicated by hysteria [female madness]." Wakefield's Irishness did not compromise her respectability. Even so, Maynard deeply feared Wakefield's passionate nature because they were "both capable of extreme excitement in faith and love."[36] We recall that when Maynard offered to free Wakefield from their committed bond in 1902, Wakefield had "kissed [Maynard] saying, 'free for this?' [Maynard] felt as 'desperate' for kissing."[37] We may propose that Maynard's feelings in the fin de siècle were a multi-layered and complex mixture of religion, science, race, and sex feeling.

What about the early decades of the 1900s? We should further explore the meaning behind Maynard's closing remarks in 1917: "I give thanks for what she [Wakefield] once was, but she can't do that." Why was this? Had Wakefield's research for her MA fired her inability to forgive their past? It seems so. In fact, Wakefield's allusion to Maynard in her MA, "Ownership in Relation to Character" (1917), was to this researcher as crucial a find as Maynard's newsletter. As mentioned, early studies in the mental (like Maynard's Tripos) were philosophical in focus on human thought. Maynard also read Darwin's *On the Origin* at Girton to debate "evolution and species." But Wakefield's "Ownership" introduced Darwinism to debate the nuances of submissive-dominant *human* relations. Then an alluring section entitled, "A Psychological Analysis of Ownership: Desire," almost provoked Maynard's earlier self-vision of a Minotaur who devoured the subjugated Irish maiden. Wakefield proposed that "a self-assertive personality" could force another to inculcate their views, even if "the controlled" suffered under them: "She [Wakefield] *says* that someday she'll have to tell me what her recent work really means," Maynard sadly wrote, "though it will hurt me."[38]

Since Wakefield gained her degrees from the University of London, we might assume her connections to the professors Karl Pearson and Charles Spearman who, historians note, shaped British psychology during the 1900s. Both scientists were influenced by Darwin's half-cousin, Francis Galton who pioneered eugenics and explored such mental processes as cognition and memory. However, Wakefield's MA did not mention these men. To support her theory of ownership and control, she drew upon specific ideas from the philosopher Georg Wilhelm Friedrich Hegel, who debated people's need for self-confirmation from others; the pioneer of psychology William James, who analyzed the consequence of human action; the psychologist William McDougall, who outlined how one's "character" shaped their relations with others; and the psychologist C. Lloyd Morgan who, like Hegel, James, and McDougall, surmised that character formation and action had outcomes; for example, individuals (like Maynard) aware of their own power could use it to control their own wellbeing.[39] It seems that Wakefield's MA exampled the shift towards examining the "psychology of the individual" constituted around the pathological; Maynard's self-assertive personality enabled her to control others.

Certainly, we glean insight into Maynard's confusion during a time of radical change in studies on the human psyche. And in another dramatic turn in 1918, and again, in 1920, Maynard's green book mentioned but did not elaborate upon conversations about psychology with Wakefield. Wakefield was apparently talking to mutual friends about the "merits of Psycho-analysis." Possibly, she knew of the Viennese pioneer of psychoanalysis, Sigmund Freud, whose influential *Three Essays on the Theory of Sexuality* (1905) had been translated into English in 1914. *Theory of Sexuality* presented some of Freud's most famous ideas, including the stages of psychosexual development, polymorphous sexuality, and what became his well-known thoughts on aggression, ambivalence, and sublimation. In the Introduction, we drew from *Theory of Sexuality* Freud's vision of how an "abnormal" ascetic upbringing (like Maynard's) could enable "excessive sexual excitations to find other outlets if, in the course of development, some [were] submitted to the process of repression."[40] Historians accede that few English intellectuals knew of psychoanalysis before the 1920s and so, Wakefield's interest in it seems as rare as Maynard's Tripos was in 1872. Still, we cannot determine who and what Wakefield read; the historian Nikolas Rose, for example, outlines various adaptions of Freudian theories that evolved after the late-1800s.[41] Whatever the case, Maynard was so traumatized by Wakefield's turn to psychoanalysis that she did not see her again until 1923.

Maynard's Textual Environment

As Maynard's green book fell silent about Wakefield in the early 1920s, her autobiography took up the reins to convey *how* she constructed her life-writing. Throughout this book we have explored Maynard's textual environment: the role and purpose of her diaries, letters, autobiography, and such publications as *Cultivation of Intellect*. Take, for example, the ways she confronted Girton's split. Her green book defended her action against free thought because they "spread disbelief," but also disclosed that her acts were driven by jealousy and revenge. Her autobiography meanwhile justified sorting "the good" (Bible study) from "the bad" (freethought) yet ultimately admitted: "I cared more about my religious ambitions than [Girtonians] themselves."[42] Let us now turn to when and how the intriguing "new psychoanalysis" shaped the elderly Maynard's thoughts.

In 1919, as Wakefield explored the "merits of Psycho-analysis," Maynard's autobiography metamorphosed into painful exhortations about "inner turmoil of feelings;" a language that seemed psychoanalytical-like. In fact, two years earlier, she had told readers: "I [Maynard] now recognize that my Tripos was the beginnings of psychology." She also mentioned her "*discomfort*" over passion with Amy Mantle at Girton and claimed to tell Mantle in 1875 (though nothing is written about it in the green book).[43] What does seem clear, however, is the increasing influence of Wakefield's scientific interests upon Maynard. If we follow Magnússon's advice and step into the metanarrative, we may contextualize Maynard's thoughts about "inner turmoil" in 1919. We first glean a post-World War I Britain eager to re-establish traditional norms in face of new discourses about gender and sexuality. The renewed emphasis on the nuclear heteronormative family encouraged women to leave jobs in offices, shops, and factories for men returning from war. Meanwhile, postwar giddiness manufactured the flapper who danced, smoked, and flirted with sexual emancipation that frightened traditionalists who thought that women in general, were out of control.

At the backdrop of this tumultuous time lay Havelock Ellis's theory of non-heterosexuality as a biological anomaly that would entrench the idea of female domesticity. Ellis's influence was clear in Freud's *Theory of Sexuality* which outlined his theory of sexual development: successful familial socialization led to a "fully mature" (heterosexual) personality, but an "arrested" stage might create the "thwarted sex instinct" or sexual problems in later life.[44] Public events that reflected the new theories of sex relayed the slow shift in ideas about female sexuality: Maud Allen's trial in London in 1918 was widely reported, and changes towards female–female passion were illustrated by attempts to make homosexual acts between women illegal in 1921.[45] As a pioneer student in mental and moral thinking, Maynard is remarkable as a woman who had claimed to feel discomfort over her same-sex intimacy since 1875.

If the autobiography mentioned "inner turmoil" in 1919, one might assume the green book would also contain hints of psychoanalytical thinking. However, the green book had been virtually silent since Maynard cut off communication with Wakefield in 1920. When it did resume in 1923, Maynard recounted her stormy reunion with Wakefield: "She [Wakefield] said, 'You did not see the harm you were doing me. When you thought that you were opening my mind, you were repressing me.'" Even angrier about how Maynard had controlled her (than when she wrote her MA), Wakefield told Maynard: "I have lived all my life under repression and tyranny, and so the charms of freedom are endless!" Psychoanalysis had impelled Wakefield to re-question morality and feel a sense of integration rather than division.[46] Maynard did not elaborate upon their conversation in her green book that, once again, fell silent about love and psychology. We recall that when her green book had suddenly resumed in 1901, it continued (as her early green book had) to merge piety with feelings of love. Since it was technically a religious diary, one wonders if Maynard ceased writing it when she questioned her religious-based views on same-sex passion. Was this easier than confronting the nature of her desire? Her late green book was certainly silent during her crises over the "mental" and sexuality.

Meanwhile, psychoanalytical ideas re-entered Maynard's autobiography as abruptly as "inner turmoil" had. In 1926, she suddenly exclaimed: "*Today*, psychoanalysts would call my college friendships 'a thwarted sex instinct!' This idea is extremely disagreeable. All I know is that I had a hunger which needed satisfying like the need for food."[47] Maynard had mulled her early years at Westfield and perhaps read (or Wakefield suggested she read) Sigmund Freud's recent *The Ego and the Id* (1923), which argued that a thwarted sex instinct could result from the child's ambivalence towards the same-sex parent. Yet even in 1918, Maynard had told readers: "Mother repressed me!" In 1925, she angrily exclaimed: "*Mother* did me *untold* mental damage!"[48] In 1927, she sadly confessed that "the early years [at Westfield] seemed okay. Then after 1886 came 'wrong excitements.' Why did I not consult someone?" Her concluding thoughts, however, challenged psychoanalysis: "If my craving *did* stem from 'repressed sex feelings,' then *why* didn't my thoughts ever stray to a man?'"[49] Maynard had consistently assured readers that she only understood "sex feeling in relation to men," but we might wonder if her challenge of psychoanalysis deflected her admission to "wrong [same sex] excitements." After all, the late 1920's cultural milieu was far removed from her late-Victorian world that had embraced female friendship within the context of heteronormativity.

Nevertheless, Maynard's Tripos and love–hate interest in thinkers like James surely gave her more insight into psychology than most. Historians of science propose that the long-term significance of psychoanalysis lay in fostering alternative forms of understanding about the self and sex. Whether Maynard read Wakefield's MA in 1917 is unclear, but she did mention "repression" in 1918; and in 1919, mentioned "inner turmoil" and "discomfort" over same-sex passion. She seemed to know psychoanalytical theories before she claimed in 1926. We cannot thus be surprised that by 1928 her autobiography couched same-sex "recklessness" more directly in psychoanalytical terms: "When the natural channel is blocked, there must be some outlet;" again, "I realize that I did not really know what craving for human love meant;" and in a later discussion, "I dare not look back on my reckless satisfying of passion. I mention love, I analyze, abstractly, but I will *not* discuss my feelings for her [Wakefield] further."[50] Maynard's "shame" about "reckless satisfying of passion" is notable. It seemed reminiscent of her "humiliation" over "misuse of passion" following Wakefield's MA about "the forceful individual" who desired and owned the "other."[51]

We might propose that Maynard's interactions with Wakefield in 1917, and after, proffer unique insights into how two late-Victorian women fought to understand the new meaning of "character," conduct, and its consequences. As we recall, Maynard at Westfield in the late 1890s associated character-building and conduct with piety, nation, and morality. Now, in 1928, she struggled with new understandings of some aspects of character traits as pathological; one outcome of "character pathology" was the tendency to form "abnormal" intimate relations. It was at this time that scientists debated "sadistic aspects of the sexual instinct." In Freud's account, the individual who failed to "fend off their strong homosexual attachment" to a loved one might become a "dangerously aggressive" lover.[52] European men of science devised biological theories of "irregular" same-sex sexual attraction rather than treat "the condition," as their American counterparts did. Forms of resistance to the cultural clime, such as novelist activist Radclyffe Hall's *Well of Loneliness* (1928), boldly advocated for female homosexual tolerance. Maynard, who read Hall's book, declared it "sad."[53] It is perhaps telling that two years later her autobiography lost momentum when she covered 1902, the year that Wakefield had suffered her second breakdown.[54] It remained unfinished at her death in 1935 (Fig. 6.3).

"Confess My Faults"

Remarkably, on 30 January 1934, Maynard aged eighty-four suddenly exclaimed in her green book: "It has been though I *could* not write this book;" entries had indeed been scant before and after she ceased writing her autobiography in 1930. Astonishingly, this time, she took up psychology where the autobiography had left off. In fact, Maynard's courage to preserve the development of her thoughts on same-sex sexual feelings was truly astounding. We might even propose she carved her own history of sexuality. She wrote: "I read over my autobiography written during 1915–1918. It all seems so new to me, as if it is about the life of someone else. I look on with a sort of compassion … I was in the 'full tide' of youth."[55] The older more empathetic Maynard—with the insight of psychoanalysis—appeared to read her "'full tide' of youth" as a burgeoning same-sex sexual consciousness. We recall that relatively few (mostly intellectual) people knew of psychology in the 1920s. Moreover, the term lesbian coined in the early 1920s still had a powerful negative stigma attached to it. Most women in the 1940s viewed lesbians as "other," whether they felt same-sex desire or not.[56] For her part, Maynard bravely continued her thoughts on 8 February:

Fig. 6.3 Constance Maynard aged eighty-five, 1934. Courtesy of Queen Mary University of London Archives/ Westfield College/ WFD. Reference WFD/25/1/1.

as I go on it gets worse and worse—I ruined it by 'falling in love' … and then, after a period of sore desolation came Marion Wakefield. It was wrong, yes, all wrong! Oh! If only I could have given that love, that preoccupation of the heart, to Christ alone! As I pursue the track, I see loss, waste and confusion around me.[57]

Maynard once again did not dwell on these thoughts in her green book. After all, it was a religious record, and so, she wished only to link her "preoccupation of the heart" to sin. Yet we might detect her deep frustration over opportunities lost. Did she think late Victorians' comprehension of women as sexually naïve, even asexual, was a loss of sorts?

The eighty-four-year-old Maynard's re-examination of her autobiography had a profound impact upon her. The green book perhaps in tribute evolved into a record of disclosure. On 24 May 1934—ten months before her death on 26 March 1935—Maynard decided "to confess [her] faults" to Wakefield, now aged fifty-nine. This was probably the first time she had apologized (or recorded her apology) to a former lover rather than explaining her mistakes through deflection, faith, the failings of others, or the culture. When first seeing Wakefield, a shocked Maynard exclaimed: "Her beautiful hair is gone! Her close-cropped head shows its small and defective shape; she is plain enough, even repulsive." Wakefield likely symbolized the "flapper" who wore short hair and dispensed of such late-Victorian customs as chaperones or female piety. Or did Maynard once again default to Wakefield's Irishness in her implicit use of "defective?" The Irish remained "under" the English.[58] The Calvinist Boers believed themselves "chosen" through the pagan African indigenous, and Maynard seemingly adopted sovereignty over the psychologically minded Irish Wakefield. Nonetheless, Maynard's ensuing apology and impassions about Wakefield were a sad read:

> The memories she wakes in me are overwhelming. For only a moment the door was opened between us, for the sight was too painful. I just said, "I suppose I missed my vocation, for I was *too* lonely. It was a blank starvation for love. Oh, Marion, forgive!" She threw herself upon me in tears, saying, "how can you say that? Look at the good!" That was all. It was if I dared not enter on those years of starvation and my reckless satisfying of it.[59]

One wonders if Wakefield's tears symbolized Maynard's admittance to their past longings as same-sex preference. Perhaps her confession helped to quell Wakefield's anger and conflict about their past.

We might suspect that psychoanalytical theories did not resonate easily with Maynard's experience of loving women. Or we might argue that even at Girton, Maynard explored her inner impulses and expressed them through (what seemed to be) unusual language. But we cannot fully know because her world is unfamiliar to us. Certainly, elements of Victorian legacy remain; for example, women globally do not always receive the same pay as men and endure disrespect at the workplace. But we might wonder who or what inspired Maynard to appropriate "electric thrills" to explain her desire for Hetty Lawrence; to subvert familial husband-mother roleplaying with Amy Mantle; or adapt discourses of Hellenist-Christianity and flora to characterize her relations with Marion Wakefield. Possibly, in the latter case, Maynard knew of emergent language(s) of late-Victorian homoeroticism. Whatever the case, "singularizing" Maynard has highlighted her unique, complex process of accepting and rejecting the new scientific discourses of sex. Her struggle at these social bridge(s) of change should not be underestimated.

We better recognize that Maynard's conception of sexuality was markedly different from that of the following generation of women such as Radclyffe Hall. She could not have perceived her lifestyle choice as a cover for her desire, as it became for twentieth-century lesbian women. Her archives relay her incredible mediation of faith, career, and love under one institutional roof. We must applaud her gains for women. The success of Westfield was due to her intellectual ability, her leadership skills, and her tenacity. These qualities were evident in her refusal to compromise, and in her fierce determination to first provide for English women university degrees. Her dedication to this goal challenged the sexist disregard for women's education in society, and even impassioned her difficult relations with Westfield Council. Maynard did not suffer from what James might call, religious-based "irrationality." In fact, his idea of one's "religious, material, and social selves" evinced aspects of her fluid self-formation in her remarkable search for sexual self-fulfillment.

"Speaking the Truth in Love, Dear"

Maynard's experiences have required us to open doors to unexpected voices that might disturb us. It has been difficult to assess her mindset. Could we discern when she spoke back to culture, or challenged it? Could we tell when she adopted self-censure or deliberately misled readers? Not always. But I do think that Maynard wished to offer us a glimpse into a past that ceased to exist; after all, as she advised her biographer Catherine Firth: "Speaking the truth in love, dear, and don't forget the love. What I shared with others must be shared and not hidden."[60] Firth could not oblige her old friend due to social ambivalence about lesbianism when she wrote in the 1940s.

Historiography today does, however, encourage nuanced analyses of past mentalité in ways that perhaps Maynard never intended. I *hope*, therefore, that she would applaud my "sharing" her life with readers and appreciate my attempts to neither judge nor classify her. Of course, all historiography is partisan, and we have noted mine in places. Nor should I get ahead of myself. If writing, interpretation, methods, and theories have "a point of view," how might Maynard assess *my* assessment of her mistakes? I would hope that she would think them kind, possibly interesting, or even amusing. But she would likely tell me that I did not fully understand them. She might, for example, criticize my inability to conceive the complexity of her struggle with faith, for I did not witness her upbringing or have her background in theology. Nor could I understand her sexual experiences and scientific studies during a period in flux; indeed, the bevy of information at my fingertips gave me the advantage of hindsight. So, I might counter Maynard with the best argument I have. I would tell her that her archive has brilliantly shared her unusual experiences as an educational pioneer. I would tell her how much I appreciated learning about her complex thought processes and distinct struggles; that her resistance to historical misogyny helped all women; and that her tackle of the shocking new ideas of the subconscious was both brave and extraordinary.

I hope, also, that Maynard would recognize and support the various skills that historians should cultivate to undertake history, at least in the traditional evidence-based sense. From Maynard's and other primary source records, we derived facts to proffer arguments about her upbringing (that she admitted was somewhat unusual) and her experiences (that did seem somewhat atypical). We did so to conceive the relevance of small events in her life that, while Maynard called mistakes, led to important life-changing decisions in her life. Historians today inform readers of their approach and their interpretation of facts and place their topic in a historical context. To fabricate or suppress facts does of course attack the fundamental integrity of history as a discipline.

In the Introduction, we discussed the importance of striving to understand what the creators of sources thought and intended, and above, I attempted an imagined conversation with Maynard. Although she left behind a huge archive, my imagined conversation (and chapters in this book) illustrate that a mass of information does not make a historian's job "easy" or easier than examining fragments of evidence. The skill is discovering amongst thousands of pages not simply facts, but the obscure, which contributes to new knowledge about the past (that perhaps Maynard hoped to convey). Maynard's "mistakes" are inestimable not only because they were never publicly known. They revealed one individual's conflicts that perhaps others like her experienced; conflicts that could open to us "another" Victorian world. Hopefully, thus, readers better understand Maynard and her struggles refracted as they were through the lens of her life.

Speaking of lenses, as historians of higher education, female sexuality, empire, and science might say, Maynard's mistakes highlight that female *experience* is not simply an add-on to history. It *is* history in its contribution to the past. Historians including myself find liberation in examining a past through the lens of historical fields, genres, incident analysis, the evidential paradigm, the linguistic turn, and queer theory. These tools of analysis remind us that while we can never know past language, they inspire more subtle ways of analyzing a past.[61] If all authors judge and construct their accounts of the past, what about Maynard? How did she sum her life experiences at the end of her life? In perhaps an analogy typical to her, she "*reckoned* that [she] could spend hours of resentment and tears recalling 'pain's most cruel sawing.'" She faced troubling burdens in both professionalism and love. At the same time, she never let go of either. In 1933, she proudly told us: "After the University preserved a silence … for some 53 years," we can now "write the letters MA after our names." If alive today, Maynard might appreciate the organization of English Heritage, London, UK, for considering honoring her as "a famous person" alongside mostly men.[62] As for "human love," the elderly Maynard wrote shortly before her death: "Alas! *it* can melt like snow in the sun unless we catch it and keep it!"[63] Unless we catch it and keep it? We cannot know with certainty what Maynard did, or why she did it, but then, imagination and speculation are inevitably part of the historian's craft. Our conclusions must necessarily be provisional and subject to revision. If a work of history is never really finished, a historian's work does end if the historian feels that they have best answered the questions they set out to answer.

Notes

1. *Budget Newsletter,* VII, 1904.
2. William James, *The Varieties of Religious Experience: A Study in Human Nature* (London: Longmans, Green, 1902), 33. Psychology emerged as its own discipline at this time.
3. *Budget* VII 1904. Wakefield's relationship with Armitage lasted just over two years.
4. *D*, 13 October 1874, 67.
5. *GB*, 24 March 1935, 55.
6. *A*, V, 44, "Westfield 1882," 3, written in August 1926. As mentioned, the pioneer of psychoanalysis, Sigmund Freud, introduced the idea of the "thwarted sex instinct" that could cause the individual's "deviant" same-sex sexual longings (Crozier, "Taking Prisoners," 450).

7. Smith, *Between Mind and Nature*, 185.
8. For more, see Wilson, *History in Crisis?* 76; and Ginzburg, "Two or Three Things," 10–35.
9. *Budget* VII 1904; William James, *Religious Experience*; and see also William James, *Principles of Psychology* (New York: Dove, 1950).
10. See Wallach Scott, "Gender: Useful Category," for more on social construction.
11. See *Budget* VII, 1904; and VIII 1906.
12. See *A*, III, 11, "1872," 392, written in November 1915; and *D*, 17 July 1904, 55.
13. *D*, 28 July 1872, 130–131; and *Budget* VII 1904.
14. *GB* December 1904, 66.
15. See *Budget* VII 1904; and *GB* 28 December 1904, 66.
16. See *GB*, 31 December 1904, 88; and 31 December 1923, 112. Constance Louisa Maynard, *The Prophet Daniel & Other Essays* (London: Morgan and Scott, 1914); and see also, for example, Constance Louisa Maynard, *The Perfect Law of Liberty* (London: Religious Tract Society, 1913).
17. See *GB*, 31 December 1925, 23; Bebbington, *Evangelicalism*, 75–105; and deVries, "No Paradoxes to Offer," in *Women, Gender and Religious Cultures*, eds., Morgan and deVries, 189–210.
18. *GB*, 19 February 1927, 104.
19. See, *GB*, 20 December 1914, 45; and 12 July 1917, 96. Maynard spoke regularly at Belstead, Girton and Westfield after her retirement. She was always expected to address faith and science.
20. *D*, 28 May 1896; and 22 January 1906.
21. *D*, 5 June 1915, 99.
22. Maynard, *Cultivation*, 9–10.
23. Sigurður Gylfi Magnússon, "Views into the Fragments: An Approach from a Microhistorical Perspective," *International Journal of Historical Archaeology* 20, 1 (2016), 182–206.
24. For more on postmodernism and queer theory, see Butler, *Gender Trouble*, vii; Beasley, *Gender & Sexuality*, 162–65; and Iggers, *Historiography in the Twentieth Century*, 134–141. See Hayden White, *Metahistory: The Historical Imagination in Nineteenth Century Europe* (Baltimore: John Hopkins Press 1973), 2, 43; and Michel Foucault, *Discipline and Punish: The Birth of the Prison* (New York: Pantheon Books, 1975).
25. In his "Views into the Fragments," 182–206, Magnússon argues that researchers should focus on the full range of "many voices" in an archive for deeper understanding of the subject.
26. *GB*, 22 October 1904, 267.
27. *GB*, 30 December 1910, 315.

28. See Smith, *Between Mind and Nature*, 17; and Collins, "England," in *History of Psychology*, ed., Baker, 182–210.
29. *GB*, 18 September 1917, 80. Royal Holloway College, London, was established in 1886, four years after Westfield. It became a School of the University of London in 1900.
30. See Vicinus *Intimate Friends*, xx, 98–108; Prins, "Greek Maenads," in *Victorian Sexual Dissidence*, ed., Richard Dellamora, 43–81; and Roden *Same-Sex Desire*, 43, 207–217.
31. *GB*, 30 December 1917, 315.
32. See *GB*, 16 April 1866, 192; 21 April 1872, 121; 7 March 1874, 90; and the latter quote in *A*, VII, "Thüringen Wald," 1897," 401, 411, written in 1929, which was copied from the *GB*, written in May 1897.
33. Current scholars, for example, classify a wide range of sadomasochistic behaviors from playful finger biting to sadomasochistic torture (see, for example, Melvin Lansky and Andrew Morrison, eds., *The Widening Scope of Shame* [Hillsdale: The Analytic Press], 1997).
34. Rose, *Psychological Complex*, 2–7. See also Leslie S. Hearnshaw, *A Short History of British Psychology 1840–1940* (London: Hodder & Stoughton, 1979).
35. For Foucault see Popkin, *Herodotus to H-Net*, 136 (taken from Foucault's *Discipline and Punish*, 1975). In Hayden White's opinion: "When it came to choosing among alternative visions of history, the only grounds for preference were either *moral* or *aesthetic* (*Metahistory* 2, 433).
36. *GB*, 20 February 1902, 117; and *A*, VII, 67, "Lent Term 1902," 446, written in May 1929.
37. *GB*, 12 April 1901, 9; 17 April 1902, 12; 20 May 1902, 116; and 16 October 1903, 76.
38. Marion E. Wakefield, "Ownership in Relation to Character," M.A. in Philosophy, Royal Holloway College, London, 1917, 29–52, accessed online from Holloway College archive. For Maynard, see *D*, 20 October 1873; and *GB*, 18 September 1917, 80.
39. The German Georg Wilhelm Friedrich Hegel based some of his ideas on 'désir' (longing, desire, and wish). William James who authored *Varieties of Religious Experience*, argued that human action from interests helped to transform the world. The British/American psychologist William McDougall, who argued that the mind had a physiological base, devised a picture of instincts that determined conduct. The British zoologist and psychologist C. Lloyd Morgan was among those who devised methods for objective description rather than analyzing experience (Collins, 'England', in *History of Psychology*, ed., Baker, 182–210; and, Bunn, Lovie, and Richards eds., *Psychology in Britain*, 42.)
40. Freud, *Theory of Sexuality*, 103–104. See also, Crozier, "Taking Prisoners,"450.
41. Rose, *Psychological Complex*, 181–193.

42. See *GB*, 6 June 1875, 176; 22 June 1875, 182; and *A*, III, 20, "My Girton Years 1875," 610, written in June 1916.
43. *A*, III, 25, "My Last Term, 1875," 763, written in July 1917.
44. For post war, see Ruth R. Pierson, *Women and Peace: Theoretical and Historical Perspectives* (London: Croom Helm), 1987. See Ellis, *Sexual Inversion*; and Freud, *Three Essays*. As mentioned, both Ellis and Freud believed individuals were born bisexual that became socially formed into heterosexual feelings, but "sexual frustration" led some to "inversion."
45. *GB*, 30 December 1923, 260. Allen was on trial for "unnatural" passion with women. See also Deborah Cohler, "Sapphism and Sedition: Producing Female Homosexuality in Great War Britain," *Journal of the History of Sexuality* 16, 1 (2007), 68–94.
46. *GB*, 30 December 1923, 260. See also Lloyd, "Religion, Same-Sex Desire," 53–73.
47. *A*, VII, 44, "Westfield 1882," 3, written in August 1926.
48. Compare Sigmund Freud, *The Ego and the Id*, 1923, trans., by Joan Riviere (New York: W.W. Norton & Company, 1960), 26–28, with *A*, II, 4, "Adolescence 1865–66," 59, written in April 1925.
49. See *A*, VII, 52, "4th Session, 1886," 174, written in May 1927.
50. See *A*, VII, 59 "Long Vacation 1895," 367, written in March 1928; and VII, 64, "Holy Land 1900," 453, written in January 1930. For science see Smith, *Between Mind and Nature*, 185.
51. Wakefield, "Psychological Ownership," 29–52.
52. Freud, *Ego and Id*, 41.
53. *GB*, 13 December 1928, 66.
54. Compare *GB*, 13 October 1902, 98; with *A*, VII, 67, "Lent 1902," 445, written in May 1930.
55. *GB*, 30 January 1934, 255.
56. See Porter and Hall eds., *Facts of Life*; and Kingsley Kent, *Making Peace*.
57. *GB*, 8 February 1934, 256.
58. *GB*, 24 May 1934, 261; and *Travel Diary* 1900. For more on empire, see Burton and Ballantyne eds., *Bodies in Contact*, 1–4; and for Ireland, see Heyck and Veldman, *Peoples of British Isles*, 562.
59. *GB*, 24 May 1934, 261. For Calvinism, see Du Toit, "Chosen People," 927.
60. Firth, *Constance Louisa Maynard*, 5.
61. For women's history see Smith-Rosenberg "Hearing Women's Words," in *Historians on History*, ed., John Tosh, 1–15; and for theories historians use see Wilson, *History In Crisis?* 117–118.
62. "Woman Waited 53 Years for Her M.A.," *Daily Mirror* (London), 16 October 1933, 4. For English Heritage, UK, which considered honoring Maynard as "a famous person" with a plaque on the original Westfield, see https://www.english-heritage.org.uk/visit/blue-plaques/
63. *GB*, 6 September 1934.

Bibliography

Unpublished Primary Sources

King, Mary. *Reminiscences of the Maynard Family, 1837-1901*, Special Collections, Courtesy of Queen Mary University of London Archives/Constance Maynard.

Maynard, Constance Louisa. Green Books, 1866-1935. Special Collections, Queen Mary University of London Archives, London. Copies of Maynard's unpublished personal documents are also available on microfilm at Wayne State University, Detroit, Michigan and the University of Toronto, Toronto, Ontario. In May 2012, Maynard's green book and autobiography were digitized at Queen Mary, University of London Archives. For access, visit, http://www.library.qmul.ac.uk/archives/digital/constance_maynard.

Maynard, Constance Louisa. Daily Diary, 1886a-1935. Special Collections, Queen Mary University of London Archives, London.

Maynard, Constance Louisa. Unpublished Autobiography, 1915-1927. Special Collections, Queen Mary University of London Archives, London.

Maynard, Constance Louisa. Budget Letters, 1887-1899. Special Collections, Queen Mary University of London Archives, London.

Maynard, Constance Louisa. Travel Diary, 1886b. Special Collections, Queen Mary University of London Archives, London.

Minutes of Council. Special Collections, Queen Mary University of London Archives, London.

Westfield College *Alumnae, Reminiscences and Memorabilia*. Special Collections, Queen Mary University of London Archives, London.

Published Primary Sources: Books and Articles

Bain, Alexander. *The Senses and the Intellect*. New York: D. Appleton, 1855.
Baines, Thomas. *Explorations in South-West Africa*. London: Longham, Green, 1864.
Biss, Irene. *Reminiscences 1907-1911*. London: Hodder, 1921.
Burstall, Sarah. *Retrospect and Prospect: Sixty Years of Women's Education*. London: Longmans, Green, 1933.
Clarke, Edward. *Sex in Education*. Boston: James Osgood, 1873.
Cavendish, Caroline. *Aims for Higher Education*. London: Simmons and Botten, 1881.
Davies, Emily. *Thoughts on Some Questions Relating to Women, 1860-1908*. Cambridge: Bowes and Bowes, 1910. Reprint, New York: Kraus, 1971.
Mill, John Stuart. *Autobiography*. New York: Columbia Press, 1924. Originally published in 1873.
Mill, John Stuart. *A System of Logic: Ratiocinative and Inductive*. London: John W. Parker, 1843.
Ellis, Havelock. *Sexual Inversion, Studies in the Psychology of Sex Volume* II, 3rd ed. Philadelphia: F. A. Davies, 1915.
Irving, Edward. "On the Humanity of Christ." *The Morning Watch*, 1 (1829): 400-421.
James, William. *The Varieties of Religious Experience: A Study in Human Nature*. London: Longmans, Green, 1902.
Linton, Eliza Lynn. *The Autobiography of Christopher Kirkland*, 3 vols. London: Routledge and Sons, 1883.
Lumsden, Louisa Innes. *Yellow Leaves: Memories of a Long Life*. Edinburgh: William Blackwood, 1933.
Maudsley, Henry. "Sex in Mind and Education." *Fortnightly Review* 21 (1874): 466-483.
Maynard, Constance Louisa. *Between College Terms*. London: James Nisbet, 1910.
Maynard, Constance Louisa. *We Women: A Golden Hope*. London: Morgan and Scott, 1913.
Maynard, Constance Louisa. *The Cultivation of the Intellect*. London: Westfield College, 1888.
Maynard, Constance Louisa. *The Prophet Daniel & Other Essays*. London: Morgan and Scott, 1914.
Maynard, Constance Louisa. "A Nation of Children, or Impressions of a Fortnight in Pondoland." *The South African Pioneer*, 10 (1897): 151-171.
Mulock Craik, Dinah. *A Woman's Thoughts about Women*. London: Hurst and Blackett, 1858.
Saunders, Frederick. *About Women, Love and Marriage*. London: Hodder, 1868.
Spencer, Herbert. *The Study of Sociology* 6th ed. London: Henry S. King, 1877.

Wallace, Alfred Russel. *Wonderful Century: Its Success and Failures.* London: S. Sonnenschein, 1898.
Wakefield, Marion E. "Ownership in Relation to Character," M.A. in Philosophy, Royal Holloway College, London, 1917, accessed on-line from Holloway College archive.
Webb, Beatrice. *My Apprenticeship.* London: Longman, Green, 1926.
Zimmern, Alice. *The Renaissance of Girls' Education in England: A Record of Fifty Years' Progress* London: A. D. Innes, 1898.

SECONDARY SOURCES: BOOKS AND CHAPTERS OF BOOKS

Bebbington, D. W. *Evangelicalism in Modern Britain: A History from the 1730s to the 1980s.* Grand Rapids: Baker Books, 1989.
Beasley, Chris. *Gender & Sexuality, Critical Theories, Critical Thinkers.* London: Sage Publications, 2005.
Betensky, Carol. "Concept of Class in Victorian Studies." In *The Routledge Companion to Victorian Literature,* ed. Denis Denisoff and Talia Schaffer (London: Routledge CRS Press, 2019): 319-320.
Bratlinger, Patrick. *Dark Vanishing: Discourse on the Extinction of Primitive Races, 1800-1930.* Ithaca, NY: Cornell University Press, 2003.
Brodozki, Bella and Schenck, Celeste. *Life/Lines Theorizing Women's Autobiography, Biography and Gender.* Ithaca: Cornell University Press, 1988.
Brown, Callum. *The Death of Christian Britain.* London: Routledge, 2001.
Burke, Peter. "History of Events and the Revival of Narrative." In *New Perspectives on Historical Writing, 2nd Edition,* ed. Peter Burke (Pennsylvania: Polity Press, 2001): 283-300.
Burton, Antoinette, and Tony Ballantyne ed. *Bodies in Contact: Rethinking Colonial Encounter in World History.* Durham: Duke University Press, 2005.
Butler, Judith. *Gender Trouble.* New York: Routledge, Chapman, and Hall, 1990.
Collins, A. "England." In *The Oxford Handbook of the History of Psychology,* ed. D. B. Baker (New York, 2012): 182–210.
Collingwood, R.G. *The Idea of History.* Oxford: Clarendon Press, 1946.
Darnton, Robert. *The Great Massacre and Other Episodes in French Cultural History.* New York: Basic Books, 1984.
Davidoff, Leonore and Catharine Hall. *Family Fortunes: Men and Women of the English Middle Class, 1780-1850.* Chicago: The University of Chicago Press, 1991.
de Lauretis, Teresa. *Queer Theory: Lesbian and Gay Sexualities.* Indiana: Indiana University Press, 1991.
deVries, Jacqueline. "More Than Paradoxes to Offer: Feminism, History and Religious Cultures." In *Women, Gender and Religious Cultures in Britian, 1800-1940* ed. Morgan and deVries (New York: Routledge, 2010): 189-221.

Doan, Laura. *Disturbing Practices: History, Sexuality, and Women's Experiences of Modern War*. Chicago: University of Chicago Press, 2013.
Faderman, Lillian. *Surpassing the Love of Men: Romantic Friendship and Love between Women from the Renaissance to the Present*. New York: William Morrow, 1981.
Firth, Catherine B. *Constance Louisa Maynard: Mistress of Westfield College*. London: George Allen and Unwin, 1949.
Foucault, Michel. *The History of Sexuality, Volume 1: An Introduction*. Translated by Robert Hurley. New York: Pantheon Books, 1985.
Foucault, Michel. *Discipline and Punish: The Birth of the Prison*. New York: Pantheon Books, 1975.
Freud, Sigmund. *The Standard Edition of the Complete Psychological Works of Sigmund Freud*. Translated by Alan Tyson. London: Hogarth Press, 1955.
Freud, Sigmund. *Three Essays on the Theory of Sexuality*. Translated by James Strachey. New York: Basic Books, 1962.
Freud, Sigmund. *The Ego and the Id*, 1923. Translated by Joan Riviere. New York: W.W. Norton & Company, 1960.
Garnett, Jane. "Religious and Intellectual Life." In *The Nineteenth Century, The British Isles: 1815-1901*, ed. Colin Matthew (Oxford: Oxford University Press, 2000): 195-227.
Ginzburg, Carlo. *Clues, Myths, and the Historical Method*. Translated by John and Anne C. Tedeschi. Baltimore: Johns Hopkins Press, 1989.
Gorham, Deborah. *The Victorian Girl and the Feminine Ideal*. Bloomington: Indiana University Press, 1982.
Hearnshaw, Leslie S. *A Short History of British Psychology 1840-1940*. London: Hodder & Stoughton, 1979.
Heyck, Thomas W. *Transformation of Intellectual Life in Victorian England*. Chicago: Lyceum Books, 1982.
Heyck, Thomas W. and Meredith Veldman ed. *The Peoples of the British Isles: From 1688 to the Present 4th ed*. Chicago: Lyceum Books, 2014.
Hilton, Boyd. *The Age of Atonement: The Influence of Evangelism on Social and Economic Thought, 1785-1865*. Oxford: Clarendon Press, 1988.
Iggers, George G. *Historiography in the Twentieth Century: From Scientific Objectivity to the Postmodern Challenge*. London: Wesleyan University Press, 1997.
Jagose, A. *Queer Theory: An Introduction*. New York: New York University Press, 1996.
Ludmilla, Jordanova. *History in Practice 2nd ed*. London: Bloomsbury Academic, 2010.
Lansky, Melvin R. and Andrew P. Morrison, ed. *The Widening Scope of Shame*. Hillsdale: The Analytic Press, 1997.

Magnússon, Sigurður Gylfi, and István M. Szijártó. *What is Microhistory? Theory and Practice*. London: Routledge, 2013.
Magnússon, Sigurður Gylfi. *Emotional History and Microhistory: A Life Story of a Destitute Pauper Poet in the 19th Century*. London: Routledge, 2020.
Marcus, Sharon. *Between Women: Friendship, Desire, and Marriage in Victorian England*. Princeton: Princeton University Press, 2007.
Maynard, John. *Victorian Discourses on Sexuality and Religion*. Cambridge: Cambridge University Press, 1993.
Newsome, David. *The Victorian World Picture: Perceptions and Introspection in an Age of Change*. New Brunswick: Rutgers University Press, 1997.
Oppenheim, Janet. *Shattered Nerves: Doctors, Patients, and Depression in Victorian England*. New York: Oxford University Press, 1991.
Pierson, Ruth R. *Women and Peace: Theoretical and Historical Perspectives*. London: Croom Helm, 1987.
Phipps, Pauline. *An Atonement for Ambition and Passion: The Experiences of British Victorian Educational Pioneer, Constance Louisa Maynard 1849-1935*. PhD Diss., Carleton University, Ottawa, 2004.
Phipps, Pauline. "The Symbolic Body of the Historical Subject." In *Literary Texts and the Arts*, ed. Corrado Federici and Esther Raventos-Pons (New York: Peter Lang, 2003): 163-174.
Phipps, Pauline. *Constance Maynard's Passions: Religion, Sexuality, and an English Educational Pioneer 1849-1935*. Toronto: University of Toronto Press, 2015.
Prins, Yopie. "Greek Maenads, Victorian Spinsters." In *Victorian Sexual Dissidence*, ed. Richard Dellamora (Chicago: The University of Chicago Press, 1999): 43-81.
Popkin, Jeremy D. *From Herodotus to H-Net: The Story of Historiography*. Oxford: Oxford University Press, 2016.
Porter, Roy, and Lesley Hall. *The Facts of Life: The Creation of Sexual Knowledge in Victorian Britain, 1650-1950*. New Haven: Yale University Press, 1995.
Porter, Andrew ed. *The Oxford History of the British Empire: The Nineteenth Century*. Oxford: Oxford University Press, 2009.
Purvis, June. *A History of Women's Education in England*. Bristol: Open University Press, 1991.
Renders, Hans, and David Veltman. "The Representativeness of a Reputation: A Third Wave in Microhistory." In *Fear of Theory: Towards a New Theoretical Justification of Biography*, ed. Renders and Veltman (Leiden: E.J. Brill, 2021): 191-194.
Roden, Frederick S. *Same-Sex Desire in Victorian Religious Culture*. Basingstoke: Palgrave Macmillan, 2002.
Rose, Nikolas. *The Psychological Complex: Politics and Science in England 1869-1939*. London: Routledge & Kegan, 1985.

Sondheimer, Janet. *Castle Adamant in Hampstead: A History of Westfield College 1882-1982*. London: Westfield College, 1983.
Smith, Roger. *Between Mind and Nature: A History of Psychology*. London: Reaktion Books, 2013.
Stachniewski, John. *The Prosecutory Imagination: English Puritanism and the Literature of Religious Despair*. Oxford: Oxford University Press, 1991.
Stern, Fritz. *The Varieties of History: From Voltaire to the Present* 2nd ed. New York: Vintage Books, 1973.
Stoler, Ann Laura. *Carnal Knowledge and Imperial Power: Race and the Intimate in Colonial Rule*. Berkeley: University of California Press, 2002.
Swindburne, Richard. *The Existence of God*. Oxford: Clarendon Press, 1979.
Tosh, John ed., *Historians on History* 3rd edition. London: Routledge Taylor & Francis, 2018.
Vicinus, Martha. *Independent Women: Work and Community for Single Women 1850-1920*. London: Virago Press, 1985.
Vicinus, Martha. *Intimate Friends: Women Who Loved Women, 1778-1928*. Chicago: University of Chicago Press, 2004.
Weeks, Jeffrey. *Sex, Politics and Society*. New York: Longman Group, 1981.
Weeks, Jeffrey. *Sexuality and its Discontents: Meanings, Myths and Modern Sexualities*. New York: Routledge, 1985.
Weeks, Jeffrey. "Social Construction of Sexuality." In *Major Problems in the History of American Sexuality*, ed. Kathy Piess (Boston: Houghton Mifflin, 2002): 1-6.
Wilson, Norman J. *History In Crisis? Recent Directions in Historiography* 3rd edition. New Jersey: Pearson Education, 2014.
White, Hayden. *Metahistory: The Historical Imagination in Nineteenth Century Europe*. Baltimore: John Hopkins Press, 1973.

Articles

Camiscioli, Elisa. "Women, Gender, Intimacy, and Empire." *Journal of Women's History*, 25, 4 (2013): 138-148.
Carstens, Lisa. "Unbecoming Women: Sex Reversal in the Scientific Discourses on Female Deviance in Britain, 1880-1920." *Journal of the History of Sexuality*, 20, 1 (2011): 62-84.
Carter, Julian. "On Mother-Love: History, Queer Theory, and Nonlesbian Identity." *Journal of the History of Sexuality* 14, 1/2 (2005): 107-138.
Clark, Anna. "Twilight Moments." *Journal of the History of Sexuality*, 14, 1/2 (2005): 139-160.
Cohen, Alan. "Mary Elizabeth Barber [ne Bowker], Some Early South African Geologists, and the Discovery of Diamonds." *Earth Sciences History*, 22, 2 (2003): 156-171.

Cohler, Deborah. "Sapphism and Sedition: Producing Female Homosexuality in Great War Britain." *Journal of the History of Sexuality* 16, 1 (2007): 68-94.

Crozier, Ivan Dalley. "Taking Prisoners: Havelock Ellis, Sigmund Freud, and the Construction of Homosexuality, 1897-1951." *Social History of Medicine* 13, 3 (2000): 447-466.

Daggers, Jenny. "Transforming Christian Womanhood: Female Sexuality and Church Missionary Society Encounters in the Niger Mission, Onitsha." *Victorian Review* 37, 2 (2011): 89-106.

Du Toit, André. "No Chosen People: The Myth of the Calvinist Origins of Afrikaner Nationalism and Racial Ideology." *The American Historical Review* 88, 4 (1983): 926-952.

Eyre, Angharad. "Love, Passion, Conversion: Constance Maynard and Evangelical Missionary Writing." *Women's History Review*, 25, 1 (2016): 35-52.

Green, Nile. "Parnassus of the Evangelical Empire: Orientalism and the English Universities, 1800-1850." *The Journal of Imperial and Commonwealth History* 40, 3, (2013): 337-355.

Heggie, Vanessa. "Women Doctors and Lady Nurses: Class, Education, and the Professional Victorian Woman." *Bulletin of the History of Medicine* 89, 2 (2015): 267-292.

Jordan, Ellen. "Making Good Wives and Mothers? The Transformation of Middle-Class Girls' Education," *History of Education Quarterly* 31, 4 (1991): 439-462.

Lloyd, Naomi. "Religion, Same-Sex Desire, and the Imagined Geographies of Empire: The Case of Constance Maynard." *Women's History Review* 25, 1 (2016): 53-73.

Magnússon, Sigurður Gylfi. "Views into the Fragments: An Approach from a Microhistorical Perspective." *International Journal of Historical Archaeology* 20, 1 (2016): 182-206.

Moore, Lisa. "'Something More Tender Still Than Friendship': Romantic Friendship in Early-Nineteenth-Century England." *Feminist Studies* 18, 1 (1992): 499-521.

Moore, Alison. "Rethinking Gendered Perversion and Degeneration in Visions of Sadism and Masochism, 1886-1930." *Journal of the History of Sexuality* 18, 1 (2009): 139-163.

Otter, Christopher. "Cleansing and Clarifying: Technology and perception in Nineteenth-Century London." *Journal of British Studies*, 43, (2004): 40-64.

Pederson, Joyce Senders. "Schoolmistresses and Headmistresses: Elites and Education in Nineteenth-Century England." *Journal of British Studies* 15 (1975): 135-162.

Phipps, Pauline. "Faith, Desire, and Sexual Identity: Constance Maynard's Atonement for Passion." *Journal of the History of Sexuality* 18, 2 (2009): 265-286.

Phipps, Pauline. "Constance Maynard's Languages of Love." *Women's History Review*, 25, 1 (2016): 17-34.

Raftery, Deirdre. "The Opening of Higher Education to Women in Nineteenth Century England: 'Unexpected Revolution' or Inevitable Change?" *Higher Education Quarterly* 56, 4 (2002): 331-346.

Renick, Timothy M. "From Apartheid to Liberation: Calvinism and the Shaping of Ethical Belief in South Africa." *Sociological Focus*, 24, 2 (1991): 129-143.

Rich, Adrienne. "Compulsory Heterosexuality and Lesbian Existence." *Signs* 5, 4 (1980): 631-790.

Robertson, Lisa. "'We Must Advance, We Must Expand': Architectural and Social Challenges to the Domestic Model at the College for Ladies at Westfield." *Women's History Review* 25, 1 (2016): 105-123.

Rupp, Leila J. "Imagine My Surprise: Women's Relationships in Historical Perspective." *Frontiers* 5 (1980): 61-70.

Rupp, Leila J. "Toward a Global History of Same-Sex Sexuality." *Journal of the History of Sexuality* 10, 2 (2001): 287-302.

Scott Wallach, Joan. "Gender: A Useful Category of historical Analysis." *American Historical Review* 91, 5 (1986): 1053-1075.

Smith-Rosenberg, Carroll. "The Female World of Love and Ritual: Relations between Women in Nineteenth Century America." *Signs* 1 (1975): 1-29.

Vicinus, Martha. "'One Life to Stand Beside Me': Emotional Conflicts in First-Generation College Women in England." *Feminist Studies* 8, 3 (1982): 603-627.

Index[1]

A

Abnormal, 7, 15, 64, 135, 139, 143
  See also Thwarted sex instinct
Agency, 41, 48, 50, 59, 61, 104, 110, 129
Ambition, 3, 10, 56, 94, 131, 132, 140
Atonement, 28, 31, 40, 45n69, 64–66, 115, 118

B

Bain, Alexander, 50, 59
Beasley, Chris, 22n54
Bebbington, D. W., 5, 45n69
Belstead, 27, 32
Bias, 10, 31, 35, 81, 84, 86, 102, 103, 110, 114, 120, 132, 133
Bible study, 37, 55, 56, 66, 140

Biblicism, 5, 25, 28, 48, 53, 55, 78, 103
Bloom, 107, 108, 136
Bratlinger, Patrick, 21n41, 122n11
Butler, Judith, 16, 39

C

Calvinist, 111, 112, 114, 130
Carter, Julian, 63
The cause, 2, 4, 8, 48, 74–77, 82, 94, 101, 131
Celibacy, 64, 100, 107, 108
Character, 30, 50, 64, 101, 113, 118, 119, 121, 139, 142, 143
Chosen, 5, 22n53, 51, 111, 112, 114, 115, 145
Civilization, 30
Civilizing, 8
  See also Colonial

---

[1] Note: Page numbers followed by 'n' refer to notes.

Clark, Anna, 108
Colleges, 2, 4–8, 15, 41, 48, 49, 51, 53, 55–61, 64–66, 74–81, 84–87, 89–91, 93, 94, 96n24, 100, 106, 107, 117, 118, 130, 137, 141
Collingwood, R.G., 110, 111, 133
Colonial, 6, 8, 30, 101, 111
See also Civilizing
Conversion, 2, 8, 25, 27, 40, 48, 53, 55–67
Council, 8, 74, 77–86, 89–91, 93, 94, 100, 116, 117, 120, 132
Cultivation of Intellect, 140

D

Darnton, Robert, 36, 38, 88, 98n60
Darwin, Charles, 5–7, 13, 27, 28, 49, 50, 53, 102, 119, 138, 139
Davies, Emily, 4, 13, 19n9, 48, 49, 53, 57, 74, 76, 77, 85
Debate, 30, 38, 51, 54, 55, 60, 71n81, 74, 77, 90, 101, 103, 122n17, 137, 138
Degenerate, 31, 101, 114
Degree, 4, 48, 57, 76, 77, 79, 96n24, 115, 117, 136, 139, 146
Denial, 37
Divinity, 115–120, 130, 131
Domestic, 32, 77–81, 119
See also Girls' accomplishments
Double standard, 33, 113

E

Electric, 38, 39, 48, 63, 66, 117, 137
Elite, 3, 13, 14, 25, 39, 43n34, 43n39, 82, 94, 112, 129, 134
Ellis, Havelock, 7, 15, 37, 39, 41, 65, 66, 107, 118, 128, 141, 151n44
Englishness, 6–12, 100, 103, 109, 119, 138

Evidential paradigm, 16–17, 83, 87, 112, 148
Evil, 5, 13, 29, 30, 32, 35, 50, 51, 59, 63, 77, 101, 102, 112–114, 117, 129, 130, 132

F

Female–female, 38, 58, 60, 74, 104, 108, 109, 128, 132, 141
Femininity, 4, 9, 10, 13, 17, 19n7, 27, 33, 39–41, 60, 63, 77, 80, 94, 101, 109, 121, 129, 134
Firth, Catherine B., 2, 17, 24, 26, 28–30, 34, 86, 110, 112, 146
Foucault, Michel, 58, 98n60, 134, 138
Free thought, 53–57, 85, 103, 140
Freud, Sigmund, 7, 8, 15, 66, 129, 139, 141–143, 148n6, 151n44
Friendship, 2, 5, 15, 16, 33, 34, 37–40, 58, 60, 63, 65, 107, 108, 118, 141, 142
Function, 39, 57

G

Gabrielle, 24, 26, 36, 43n39, 114
Galton, Francis, 31, 139
Gender, 13, 16, 17, 24, 27, 33, 39, 40, 55, 58, 60, 65, 76, 81, 82, 84, 94, 97n46, 109, 113, 134, 140
Ginzburg, Carlo, 9, 10, 82, 83, 87, 111, 112
Girls' accomplishments, 4, 19n9, 27, 75, 79
Girton, 4–7, 12–16, 18, 40, 47–67, 74, 75, 77, 78, 85, 94, 102, 104, 106, 107, 110, 111, 115, 118, 128, 136, 138, 140, 145
See also Girton's split

Girton's split, 56–58, 66, 87, 104, 140
Gray, Frances, 81, 82, 87, 91–93

H
Harry, 27, 31–34, 54, 75, 100, 101, 114, 131
Henry, 13, 24, 25, 28, 30, 31, 43n34, 43n39, 75, 110–115, 123n42, 124n54
Heteronormative, 15, 39, 122n22, 136, 140
Higher learning, 4, 48, 55–57, 74, 76, 77, 79, 89, 90, 94
High schools, 74, 90–91
Historiography, 4, 11, 12, 15–17, 34, 83, 86, 94, 146
Hysteria, 77, 86, 119, 138

I
Incarnation, 118
  See also Rest in Faith
Incident analysis, 16, 36, 148
Irishness, 8, 103–109, 116–121, 122n17, 138, 145

J
James, William, 128–132, 136, 139, 142, 146, 150n39
Josephine, 24, 26, 33, 43n39, 114, 131

K
Kant, Immanuel, 50
King, Mary, 24, 26, 28–30, 34, 37, 41n3, 54

L
Labouring classes, 4, 13, 32
  See also Degenerate
Linguistic turn, 16, 88, 108, 110, 134, 148
Little flock, 55–57
Lower orders, 13, 31, 63, 114
  See also Labouring classes

M
Magnússon, Sigurður Gylfi, 10, 133, 134, 140, 149n25
Malthus, Thomas, 30, 31, 102, 113
Mantle, 8, 48, 52, 53, 60–66, 75, 90, 107, 118, 137, 138, 140, 145
Marcus, Sharon, 104
Masculinity, 8, 13, 33
Maynard, Constance Louisa, 2, 24, 48, 73, 99, 128, 140–143
  as educational pioneer, 2, 3, 12, 76, 82, 87, 147
  as missionary, 5, 57, 66, 77, 90, 119, 130
  as nationalist, 3, 8, 101, 115
  psychology, 2, 7, 9, 12, 13, 15, 18, 118, 120, 128, 129, 136, 137, 139–143
  and same-sex desire, 15, 39, 118, 135, 143
Maynard, Gabrielle (sister of CLM), 24
Maynard, Harry (brother of CLM), 31
Maynard, Henry (father of CLM), 24
Maynard, Josephine (sister of CLM), 24
Maynard, Louisa (mother of CLM), 28
Mental, 6, 50, 51, 120, 137–139, 141
Mental and moral, 7, 141

INDEX

Mentalité, 16, 57–67, 134, 146
Metcalfe, Fanny, 8, 74, 77, 82, 84–91, 93, 94, 117
    See also Metcalfe event
Metcalfe event, 81–93, 100
Microhistory, 3, 9–11, 16, 17, 58, 128, 134
Middle class, 4, 6, 13, 19n9, 24, 25, 27, 31, 37, 41n5, 75, 77, 80, 84, 90, 101, 113, 115
Mill, John Stuart, 31, 50, 59, 60, 63, 69n53
Minotaur, 104, 110, 138
Missionary, 5, 6, 57, 61, 66, 75, 83, 90, 97n43, 101, 102, 108, 119, 130, 131
Moral, 7, 24, 28, 29, 31, 50, 59, 65, 76–78, 121, 141

N

Nation, 27, 39, 40, 101, 109, 110, 143
    See also Nationalism
Nationalism, 6, 8, 25
Newsletter, 2, 12, 18n2, 100, 108, 128, 129, 131, 138

P

Pain, 8, 29, 36, 50, 64, 65, 106, 109, 148
Paley, William, 49
Phipps, Pauline, 30, 34
Physiological, 4, 31, 120, 150n39
Physiology, 25, 77, 90
Piety, 5, 6, 27, 28, 33, 38, 56, 76, 78, 100, 108, 115, 119, 141, 143, 145
Postmodernist, 134, 138
Pray, 55, 66, 118

Professionalism, 12, 74, 76, 83, 84, 86, 131, 132, 148
Prophet, 5, 6, 8, 41, 48–67, 109–111, 116–121, 130
Prophet Daniel, 130
Psyche, 3, 7
Psychoanalysis, 7, 9, 128, 129, 139–143, 148n6
Psychology, 2, 7, 9, 12, 13, 15, 18, 20n23, 60, 120, 128, 129, 136, 137, 139–143, 148n2
Psyche, 3, 7, 47, 137, 139

Q

Queer, 16, 39, 61, 63, 76, 104, 109–111, 122n22, 134, 135, 148

R

Race, 13
Religious doubt, 13, 50, 51, 54, 55, 58, 76, 94, 119
Rest in Faith, 5, 12, 28, 56
Roden, Frederick S., 104, 105, 122n22
Roleplaying, 60, 61, 63–66, 145
Rules, 26, 50, 63, 78, 79, 84, 91, 93, 114

S

Salary, 81–83, 93, 94
Secularism, 5, 29, 53, 55, 66, 94, 117, 128, 130, 135, 136
Sex, 10, 11, 15, 16, 24, 33, 36–40, 58, 60, 66, 67, 105, 107–110, 129, 135, 136, 138, 141, 142, 146
    See also Sexuality

Sexism, 77, 93
Sexology, 13, 15, 128
Sexuality, 5
Shame, 10, 29, 56, 63, 86, 107, 108, 138, 142
Smith, Adam, 30, 50, 113
Smith, Roger, 6, 60, 129
Smith-Rosenberg, Carroll, 5, 16, 22n53, 37, 58, 63
Sondheimer, Janet, 86
Sower, 123n42
Spencer, Herbert, 50, 102
Stoler, Ann Laura, 8, 109
Suffer, 40, 146

T
Thwarted sex instinct, 141, 142, 148n6

Transgress, 24, 28
Tripos, 7, 9, 12

V
Vicinus, Martha, 2, 58

W
Wakefield, Marion E., 8, 9, 12, 100, 103, 104, 106–110, 115, 116, 118–120, 123n35, 125n80, 128, 129, 135–145, 148n3
Wallace, Alfred Russel, 102, 103, 119
Weeks, Jeffrey, 22n52, 43n40, 70n76
Westfield College, 2
We Women, 4, 5, 11, 13, 43n33
Workers, 9, 13, 30, 63, 101
    See also Labouring classes